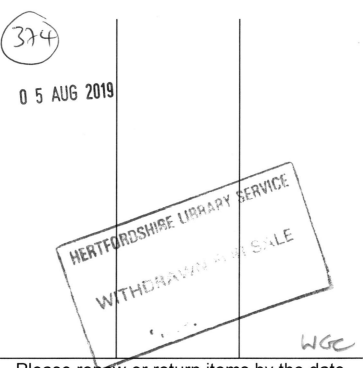
Please renew or return items by the date shown on your receipt

www.hertsdirect.org/libraries

Renewals and enquiries: 0300 123 4049

Textphone for hearing or speech impaired   0300 123 4041

Hertfordshire

Exposure Ninja

www.ExposureNinja.com
Free lifetime book updates at:
www.ProfitableSocialMediaMarketing.com/book-buyer

1

Contents

Why Social Media?

Most people in business fall somewhere between two extremes when it comes to social media:
On one side we have those who pledge allegiance to the flag of social media regardless of its potential impact on their profit. They'll spend all day tweeting, posting, sharing, hearting and whatever-else-ing because they love it. To them it's not a business activity but a social activity.

On the other extreme we have the stubborn sceptics. To them Twitter is for twits and Linkedin is like dating for the under-employed. They refuse to dip their toes in the water for fear of being drowned in time vampire notifications and wasting their lives being harassed by people they don't like.

The rest of us lie somewhere in between. Perhaps you've experimented with social media, but unsure of how to integrate it into your marketing and daily activities it got left behind and your half-finished profiles live on to haunt you about what could have been. Or maybe you've heard how important social media can be, but without knowing where to start or what to aim for, it all seems a bit overwhelming.

Whether you're new to business or an experienced marketer looking to sharpen your saw with the new tools, this book will navigate you through the process of

developing your own social media identity, incorporating the values that make your business special and give you a road map for using these components to grow your business.

We aim to prove that social media marketing doesn't just have to be about big brands with dedicated teams getting their topics trending. In fact it's actually the small and medium sized businesses who have the most to gain from a well designed social campaign. Learning lessons from the big brands and applying them to smaller businesses is the name of the game here.

We'll also aim to give you the necessary ammunition to sell social media marketing to those in your organisation who don't share your enthusiasm. They'll try to persuade you that it's a new fad - something that'll die out before long. Far from being a new fad, 'social marketing' is *the* oldest form of marketing. Conversations about their products and services have always been an important source of sales for businesses who offer something good. But until Twitter, Facebook, Pinterest & co came along, these conversations happened in private, out of sight of the companies being discussed.

Now, thanks to social media, all these conversations are happening in public and within a few clicks of anyone who wants to find them. Word of mouth can be measured, encouraged, promoted and even shaped in a more effective way than ever before. Savvy businesses can identify potential customers at their peak moment of need, not because they walk into a shop, but just because they *say* something. You and I can advertise to fans of a particular brand, product or lifestyle for just a few cents, and in less than 10 minutes. Even more significant, we can build authority and attract a targeted audience without paying a penny. This sort of opportunity has never before existed.

Critics of social media have completely missed this point, preferring to focus on the disposable and irrelevant aspects instead. They'll say things like "why would I use Twitter? I don't care what celebrities eat for breakfast". This is like saying "I don't read books because I'm not interested in trashy novels" or "I don't watch TV because I'm not interested in music videos". They're not only throwing the baby out with the bathwater, they're throwing the entire *bath* out as well.

Many businesses failed to spot potential in the early Internet for anything other than tech-geeks. Critics of the slow and noisy early automobiles failed to spot the transformation it would have on productivity and mobility over time. As with any revolutionary technology, there will be critics and people who see the potential and grab the opportunity with both hands.

So whether it's reaching potential clients, existing clients and other stakeholders in any part of the world; generating leads, or building your brand and positioning you and your business at the forefront in your market, social media, *done properly*, can be extremely profitable and effective. And nothing to do with photos of food and cats - unless you're a cat food company.

The size of the potential audience is so large it's difficult to truly appreciate. Facebook's latest report puts the number of monthly active users at 1.15 *billion*. Twitter comes in at over 500 million. Google+? 365 million.

But what's *most* exciting is not the big numbers, as very few businesses will have something that a billion people want. What's much more exciting is that these big numbers are built from millions upon millions of different niches. Whether it's Chihuahua owners, Chihauhua puppy breeders or people who dress up as Chihuahuas at the weekend; fans of high end audio, high end wine or jumping off high buildings, if your audience shares a common interest, trait or goal, you can be in front of them within seconds. It doesn't matter where they live, what they spend their time doing or the magazines they read - they're all there using social media.

And it's not just consumer businesses: Social Media channels have changed the way businesses interact with other businesses, potential investors and other stakeholders as well.

Of course there are many other reasons for getting into Social Media Marketing for your business. Most large brands are still unsure about how to deal with the customer service opportunity now that their customers can (and do) take to Twitter or Facebook to complain or praise any aspect from service to price. Many brands choose to ignore it, hoping it will go away and scared of being held to ransom by angry customers influential on social networks. But as we'll see later in the book, this 'tactic' is a wasted opportunity to sell more.

So as you can see, the potential for social media success is huge. Companies like ours regularly audit and consult with a range of businesses from around the world, and it's very rare - almost unheard of - that we'll see a market with more than a couple players using social media really effectively. Whether it's a lack of resources and know how or an unwillingness to take the risk of jumping in, your competitors are almost certainly underusing social and passing up a massive opportunity. In the land of the blind, the one eyed man is king. Getting social media right could be the most important thing you do for your business this year.

Free Gifts

As a thank you for buying this book, we'd like to offer you 2 free gifts:

Free 7-Point Online Marketing Audit

Claim a free online marketing audit by visiting www.exposureninja.com/audit

Your audit will cover the following areas:
- Free expert tips and suggestions for using social media in your market to attract more customers for your business, whether or not you're already using it
- Analysis of your website's visibility and tips to attract more traffic and boost conversions
- Competitor analysis including suggestions of opportunities to exploit

All you need to do is fill out a short form to help us understand your market, competitors and what's already working for you. One of our research team will then do the research and send your 7-point audit as a .pdf including suggestions you can implement immediately.

Free Lifetime Book Updates

Because the world of social media changes so frequently, we're constantly updating this book. In order to keep you up-to-date with the very latest we'd like to offer you free lifetime book updates.

Each time the book is updated, you'll receive an email summarising the changes, as well as the full new edition. Head to www.profitablesocialmediamarketing.com/book-buyer to claim your lifetime updates now.

About This Book

We wrote this book with one aim: to help small and medium sized businesses set up and run profitable social media campaigns.

Why the focus on small and medium sized businesses? Because they tend to have enough agility and maneuverability to test and implement new strategies without the hassle of seeking approval from different departments. Big brand social media is a different beast and often more about getting ideas approved than getting things done fast.

We believe that small and medium sized businesses (we usually define them by having 1-100 employees) are the unsung heroes of our world. From one woman startups to specialist manufacturing businesses, SMBs prop up the economy and deliver the things that really make a difference. These are typically also the businesses that can profit most from clever social media marketing because of the potential sales power of using personality and positioning.

This book is written by Tim and Tash from Exposure Ninja. Tashmeem Mirza is our Social Media manager and has run social media campaigns for numerous businesses in different markets across the world. Her 'real world' experience of social media gives her insight into the principles and commonalities that exist between a variety successful campaigns.

Head ninja Tim Kitchen's experience running Exposure Ninja and handling the online marketing for more a hundred small and medium sized businesses over the last eight years, including many of his own, has given him an understanding of marketing strategy and understanding what makes people click, read and buy.

As big fans of ROI (return on investment), everyone at Exposure Ninja believes passionately in marketing that pays for itself, and it's not uncommon for our clients to see double digit multiple return on investment within a matter of months. Ten times, 20 times and even 30 times; once you understand how to get in front of a customer and what drives them to buy, you 'unlock' your marketing and break through the barrier of always wondering where the next sale will come from.

As you can see, we are 'doers' rather than authors. We wrote this book ourselves so there are going to be places where the grammar wouldn't make our school English teachers proud*. We might start sentences with the words 'and' and 'but'. And we might write how we talk. But hopefully that doesn't distract from the message, and your thoughts while you read will be how to apply and make money from these ideas rather than how well or poorly the English is executed.

Feedback and Comments Welcome!

I really hope you've enjoyed reading this book as much as we enjoyed putting it together for you. If you have any comments, suggestions or feedback you can contact me directly tim@exposureninja.com

If you're not happy with the book in any way, I'd also like to know. I'd be happy to personally refund you the cost of the book if you don't consider it a good investment. Just drop me an email and we'll get it sorted :-)

Tim Kitchen
September 2013

Integrating Social Media Marketing in Your Business

Whether you choose to handle the social media marketing yourself or hire help in some form really depends on your business. Employing a full time social media manager can be a good option if the budget allows and they prove to be a good investment. For many businesses however, the cost of a full time employee who does only social media is likely to be unrealistic.

This leaves two options: have an existing staff member (perhaps you) take on the social media marketing, or outsource it to a specialist company.

After reading our book on SEO, many business owners decide that actually their time is better spent elsewhere in their business, whether it's focussing on their products or managing their team. They now understand enough about SEO to be able to outsource it and track the results. Some business owners on a lean budget or who are that way inclined decide to take on the SEO themselves with their new knowledge.

Similarly for social media marketing, you might decide after finishing this book that you or someone on your team can implement what you've learnt. If you have the time, this is a great solution. No one understands your business like you, and your passion will come across in your posts and interactions. You might decide that outsourcing your social media to a specialist company like Exposure Ninja is a more suitable option if you're tied up elsewhere in your business and you don't think you can spare the time.

A good third party team of Social Media experts should help you grow your brand and capture qualified leads whilst allowing you to get on with what you do best.

What exactly should your business expect from Social Media Marketing?

If you or your hired Social Media team is putting in the right amount of time and effort into profitable Social Media Marketing strategies, you should be able to accomplish the following goals (we'll look at Social Media goals in more detail later on, but here is a brief overview):

Goal 1. Directly sell more of your product or service
Generating sales and leads from Social Media Marketing begins with having clear goals in mind and defined KPIs. Once these are in place and you know what you're aiming for, we can begin to look at some specific ways to move your followers towards these goals, whether that's raising a hand to say they're interested or making the purchase.

Goal 2. Positioning your business in your market
Particularly for generic markets where the big players lack any personality, your social persona can be an excellent way to stand out by standing for or *against*

something. Whether you sell nails, washing machine spares, tax preparation or dog food, your customers are human. And people buy from people. The blander the industry, the greater the opportunity to win by injecting some personality.

Goal 3. Increase awareness amongst your target audience

This is all about targeting a relevant audience and using some clever strategies to get your message in front of them. Although an extremely worthy goal, awareness has the danger of becoming wishy washy so it's important to build in solid measurable targets as well.

Goal 4. Expose yourself to a new audience

If you are looking to branch out and begin selling to a new audience, access to an almost unlimited number of clearly defined new audiences is quicker and easier than ever. You'll find these audiences extremely eager to hear from anyone with an appealing proposition, so getting your message right is key.

Goal 5. Encourage repeat business

Generating a community around your brand is not only a good way to bring in new leads but also helps encourage repeat business through ongoing relationships with your customers. For businesses of any size, keeping in their customers' minds and being visible is incredibly valuable, and made simpler than ever by Social Media.

Goal 6. Generate referrals

With some skillful positioning and cultivated word of mouth, you can use your existing customer base to find some new targeted customers. But referrals don't happen accidentally, and the right strategy can make a big difference to your results.

Really? Sales and Leads through Social Media Marketing?

Yes really. We believe that <u>all</u> marketing should be an investment, not a cost. Social Media Marketing should earn you back more than you put in, which is why we advocate an approach which takes it from being purely a branding and awareness tool to more like a mixed marketing tool which combines elements of the traditionally 'softer' branding approach with a good dose of direct sales.

Some of the ways you can use Social Media to generate sales include:

1. Generating leads and sales from blog traffic
2. Using interaction on Facebook, LinkedIn, Twitter, Pinterest and the others to generate qualified new leads for your business through targeted posts, promoting reviews, offers and case studies
3. Increase conversion rates by demonstrating the quality of your customer service

4. Increase repeat and referral business by reaching out to your existing customers through social channels
5. Improve your search ranking by integrating social media with your website.

Big Brand Social Media Case Studies

Even for large brands with dedicated social teams social media is not an exact science, and as if to illustrate how thin the line is separating success and failure, here are some of the best (and worst) campaigns of recent times:

Nike at the Olympics 2012

During last year's London Olympics we saw Nike steal the show with its guerilla marketing tactics and leaving its competitors (including the official sponsor, Adidas) in awe.

At a time when most brands were relying heavily on celebrity endorsement it instead decided to focus on the athlete inside all of us. It bought up hundreds of billboards around the city featuring the hashtag #findgreatness. In doing so, it aligned itself with the inspirational message of the games and the feeling in viewers that actually, being more involved with sport in their lives might not be a bad thing.

Adidas on the other hand spent tens of millions of pounds to be the official sponsor and ran a campaign where it featured Team GB athletes. Although it used the hashtag #takethestage, the Social Media element wasn't as heavily integrated as Nike's campaign, and seemed more like an afterthought.

The results?

Twitter: Between July 27th and August 2nd 16,000 tweets with the hashtag #findgreatness were recorded, compared to Adidas's #takethestage which measured just 9,295.

Facebook: A recorded number of 166,718 new users joined Nike's official page during the games whereas Adidas only got 80,761 new fans. Also data from Experian Hitwise shows that Nike achieved a 6% growth in its number of Facebook fans and a 77% boost in engagement on its Facebook page compared to 2% and 59% respectively for Adidas.

Far from being 'just numbers', each of these tweets and fans represents a real person engaging with that company's advertising. These are people that are opting in to receive future marketing messages, and are willing to identify themselves with the brand. Their hashtagged tweets are free adverts pushed to their friends and contacts.

Old Spice Terry Crews

We've seen some awesome viral campaigns from Old Spice in the past. In 2012 Old Spice decided to ditch its Old Spice Character and made a viral video featuring ex-NFL player Terry Crews.

What was so special about this video? Well it had little to do with the product itself but everything to do with the brand. The video had Crews playing musical instruments by flexing his muscles, and viewers could use their keyboard to play their own music.

The video has millions of views on Vimeo and introduced Old Spice to a completely new market that perhaps would never have considered it as a relevant brand to them. What's more is that they achieved this without changing their branding, packaging or core message in a way that might interfere with their existing customer base. Just like with Nike and Adidas, the entertainment value of the video led to sharing across social networks far beyond what they brand had paid for.

Cadbury's 1 Million Fans

Cadbury has been experimenting with social media and viral advertising for a number of years and in 2012 started one of its most interesting marketing campaigns, resulting in an additional 40,000 new fans for its Facebook page.

When their fan count reached 1 million, Cadbury decided to celebrate by building a giant Facebook 'like' thumb out of pieces of Dairy Milk chocolate.

The brand used teaser ads to build up the anticipation then it live streamed in a studio decorated with user-generated content and photos. The Cadbury team was on hand to respond to user requests as well as comments in the video. In total, over 350,000 people were actively involved in the campaign

That's 350,000 people who now have a deeper association with Cadbury than any other chocolate brand, and who took time out of their day to interact and receive the marketing message.

Dumb Ways to Die

Towards the end of 2012 the Melbourne Transport Authority in Australia released a very popular and funny video that was aimed at raising awareness about railway safety. The video had a very catchy tune and at the end included a small amount of 'under the radar' preaching about railway safety. It reached 30 million views after going live for only 2 weeks, and currently has 43 thousand likes on Facebook. The accompanying website http://dumbwaystodie.com/ and Dumb Ways to Die app is well worth a look to see how a little creativity can embed public safety messages in people's heads without being boring or patronising.

How Not to Do Social Media Marketing

We've also seen some big brand disasters recently, demonstrating that even large dedicated social media teams don't always get things right. No doubt there were some sleepless nights for those involved...

McDstories

McDonalds, in the hope of sparking nostalgic thoughts of happy McDonalds memories in their audience, decided to create the hashtag "#McDstories". The brand hoped that this hashtag would get people thinking and talking about memories of good times and happy meals shared with friends and family at McDonalds. Instead this little hashtag turned into an ugly nightmare when people started sharing horror stories and gripes about the franchise's service, food, hygiene and so on.

I'm sure their social media team was definitely not loving tweets such as:

"Eating a Quarter Pounder value meal makes me feel exactly the same as an hour of violent weeping. #McDStories" - @mmemordant

and

"My father used to bring us McDonalds as a reward when we were kids. Now he's horribly obese and has diabetes. Lesson learned. #McDStories" - @natebramble

As with all social media 'bashtag' campaigns, a failure to take into consideration the negative as well as positive feelings towards a brand resulted in this undesired interpretation of a well-intentioned campaign.

American Apparel During Hurricane Sandy

Capitalising on current news stories can be risky business even when you have the best of intentions, and American Apparel makes our list for their Hurricane Sandy campaign, run in Oct 2012.

The clothing brand decided to offer a 20% discount during the Hurricane, which already risks accusations of opportunism, but their message "In case you're bored during the storm, get 20% off for the next 36 hours" wasn't very well received by the American customers huddled in basements waiting for the second costliest hurricane in American history to destroy their homes.

#WaitroseReasons

Waitrose's campaign fail might on the surface appear similar in some ways to McDonalds. However, their handling of what happened when hashtags go wild serves as an excellent lesson in reputation management. The upmarket food retailers, in a desire to get some #customerlove, decided to ask their followers to complete this sentence: "I shop at Waitrose because _____. #WaitroseReasons"

The replies that the brand received were not as good as they predicted. People mocked the brand and made fun of the 'posh' image. For example, Polly Courtney tweeted:

"I shop at Waitrose because Clarrisa's pony just WILL NOT eat ASDA Value straw. #WaitroseReasons"

While @Amoozbouche wrote

"I shop at Waitrose because it makes me feel important and I absolutely detest being surrounded by poor people #waitrosereasons"

This single tweet was retweeted 127 times, demonstrating the power of viral sharing and showing in no uncertain terms that the #waitrosereasons hashtag campaign had gotten out of hand.

But Waitrose took the responses in good humour and tweeted that they enjoyed the funny replies and thanked the audience for making them smile. This was a great way to handle a good situation turned bad, diffusing the situation and showing their human side.

Starbucks #Spread the Cheer

Starbucks has long been touted for their excellent use of Social Media to drive sales, but their presence in the fail list shows that not everyone gets it right *all* the time. Last year during the growing criticism of many big companies' tax practices in the UK, they witnessed some of the public resentment spilling out into their social media interactions.

At the height of the publicity in Christmas 2012, they decided to run an ill-advised Christmas PR campaign with the hashtag #SpreadtheCheer. This was already skating on thin ice, so their decision to display the resulting messages on a large screen in the Natural History museum in UK certainly raised some eyebrows in the social media marketing world. You guessed it...

Another hashtag disaster!

The messages that the brand received on Twitter were mostly from unhappy taxpayers voicing their opinions about the company's business practices:

"I like buying coffee that tastes nice from a shop that pays tax. So I avoid @starbucks #spreadthecheer" - @dickdotcom

@SpatchcockOfTheYard pitched in: "Tax paid: £8.6m. Additional tax paid to improve public image: £20m. Posting live tweets to a big screen: priceless.#spreadthecheer"

While other tweeters used the bashtag as an opportunity to air separate grievances:

"Starbucks' anti labor behaviors mean my good friend has to work three 12 hour shifts two days after giving birth.#spreadthecheer" - @ashponders

The lesson? It is probably a good idea to do some research on what people are saying about your brand *before* starting a campaign.

Although campaigns like this generate a significant amount of negative publicity for the brands involved, they demonstrate just how involved people become in social media that connects with them. Those who fail to see the positive potential in case studies like these are missing more than half of the picture.

Although the examples above are all for large companies, the lessons, strategies and underlying principles remain the same for businesses of any size. The high value response to reading these case studies is not "but that would never work for my business". Instead the smart business owner asks "*how* can I use that in my business?"

Planning Your Social Media Campaign

Preparation Work

Social Media marketing is still marketing, which means that any effective campaign obeys the basic principles of marketing. We define these basic principles as:

1. Finding the right **m**essage
2. Targeting the right **m**arket
3. Using the right **m**ethods of communication (advertising media)

These three principles are the difference between a social media campaign that goes viral, engages people and brings your business new traffic, awareness and customers, and one that disappears without a trace into the infinite social media ether. Wider than this, they apply to all marketing whether it's newspaper ads, Google Adwords or even finding a date or persuading your kids to tidy their rooms.

In order to give our profitable social media marketing campaign the best possible start, we'll take a look at each of these principles in turn:

Finding your right message

The key to getting the *message* of your Social Media campaign right is having a goal in mind before you start. All too often this crucial first step is left out. Either it feels too difficult, gets left until last (then forgotten) or it's completely new thinking. It's easy to just head straight to Facebook and start creating a business page, or go to twitter and start Tweeting. But setting off without a map makes it unlikely that the journey will end somewhere rewarding. Just as with any goals, you can continue to change direction and reassess where you're going once you start moving, but having *at least an idea* of where you want to end up is strongly advised before you set off.

Your goal for social media might be any of the following:

Social Media Goal 1. Directly sell more of your product or service

Selling *directly* through social media is usually reserved for niche e-commerce businesses. Their followers are likely to be fans of the sort of products they sell, so will see value in receiving sales pitches through Twitter or Facebook. Tweeting about new products in store, publishing third party reviews with a link to buy the product mentioned, promoting special offers and so on is acceptable to an audience who is extremely qualified and ready to buy.

The sorts of markets that direct sales through social media can work best tend to be extremely passionate markets where very little obvious selling is required. An example is music, where an artist promoting their latest recording or merchandise can send their fans directly to their online shop on the opening day to grab the new release. Authors sharing the Amazon page for their newly released book will have a similar success if their audience is already warm and rapport is strong.

But even in these cases, care should be taken to balance direct sales messages with 'value-add' messages, blog posts, videos and so on to avoid 'ad blindness'.

Another world in which direct sales through social media can be effective is in time-sensitive deals. When your message needs to get out quickly to your audience, social media is one of the fastest broadcast methods ever invented. Daily deals, limited quantity sales or last minute offers are all suited to direct selling through social media.

Whilst the idea of selling straight from tweets and posts can seem appealing, the danger comes when an organisation starts to believe that theirs and their audience's goals in social media are aligned. Remember that your audience is always asking "'what's in it for me?" and more often than not, the answer is not that they really want to hear more about your product. By only ever pushing out sales messages, your audience might come to feel that they are getting very little value or interest from having you constantly present in their newsfeeds. In a world of constant and relentless advertising, who actually *volunteers* to subject themselves to more?

The answer to this problem is twofold: firstly it's important to make your social media audience feel as if they are part of an exclusive club and privy to something that the rest of the general public have no access to. This might involve making them the first to know about something (useful when an offer is time-sensitive or limited availability) before the rest of the world finds out. Alternatively this feeling of exclusivity might be developed through Social Media-specific offers or releases. Bournemouth Pizza co is a small startup pizza restaurant that uses this technique fantastically; their Facebook special offers are only promoted on Facebook, and customers wishing to redeem them have to mention that they saw the offer on Facebook. This gives Facebook fans a feeling of being 'insiders' compared to regular visitors, and also tells the restaurant staff how effective their Facebook campaign is, because each Facebook-generated customer is clearly identifying themselves at the point of sale. To grow their fanbase further, they promote the Facebook page in store so customers sat waiting for their pizza, smartphone in hand, start checking out the offers. They're now 'in the herd' and will receive future marketing messages and offers, increasing the chance of a repeat visit.

The second answer to turning people off with too much advertising is through mixing the ads with interesting and valuable non-advertising content. This might be curated content likely to be of interest to your target market (covered in the next section), interesting survey results or trend info, or simply enjoyable 'fluff': consumable messages like pictures, quotes and entertaining videos. Mixing your advertising and sales messages with these interest pieces provides enough entertainment value to keep your audience, so you can then sell to them. It's not unlike a TV program with advert breaks - the program content is there to keep the audience sat on the sofa all evening to watch adverts, and make them more receptive when the ads appear. Remove the programs and nobody watches. Likewise if you remove the value from your tweets and just push out ads, your audience leaves the sofa or changes channel.

Social Media Goal 2. Positioning your business in your market

Social media is a fantastic positioning tool to show the world *where* you stand and *what* you stand for. You can then use this positioning to attract more of the customers you *want*, and put off the sort of customers you *don't want*.

Just as every business that has a clearly identified market has an ideal customer profile, they also have a group that *wouldn't* make good customers. Luxury brands seek to discourage price shoppers using expensive-looking window displays, while low cost airlines use bold bright logos and advertising to discourage luxury customers who would complain at the lack of (quality) food, the abundance of screaming children and vomit, and the boarding and unboarding 'experience'. Social Media allows you to clearly mark who you *are* and *aren't* suitable for.

This strategy can be particularly useful in crowded markets susceptible to commoditization where you want to help your audience understand the real difference between your business and your competitors, so they'll pay more for your product or service. People buy on price when all else is equal, but by clever social media positioning you can show that all else *isn't* equal. Whether your business has a strong environmental or ethical ethos (Lush Cosmetics), you're particularly customer service orientated (Zappos) or you offer the best value in your market, these are all things that might not be easy to convey during a transaction or brief introduction. But over time through a carefully considered Social Media campaign, you can build these values into your audience's consciousness.

Incidentally, of the small and medium sized businesses who ask us for help with their online marketing, it's those who lack a clear understanding of where they fit in their market and what makes them the best choice that tend to be struggling the most. If you can't clearly enunciate why a potential customer should buy from you, chances are that they won't be able to either and the transaction doesn't happen. In cases like this, a new website, big ad campaign or aggressive SEO won't make a huge difference. Until the business owner has these answers clear in their own minds, the car is being driven with the handbrake on.

The good news is that if this sounds like you, you're sitting on a huge amount of untapped potential. Once you give your customers a compelling reason to buy from you, the handbrake goes off and your marketing becomes a lot more rewarding.

Social Media Goal 3. Increase awareness amongst your target audience

Many brands who draw a blank with social media miss this crucial observation: any social media audience is essentially a collection of mini audiences publicly identifying themselves, Venn diagram-like, through their relationship (follower, liker, retweeter) with other accounts.

If your target audience is sports fans, for example, a football club's Facebook fans gives you extremely quick access to a highly qualified group of potential customers. They're sports fans, they're receptive to sports-related messages and they use social media. What about sports fans who like Range Rovers? Sports fans who like Range Rovers, with a University education, living in Spain? Every target audience is out there, it's just a case of narrowing your search and understanding the identifying traits.

There are two steps here:

1. Understanding your audience, and
2. Finding more of them.

The more you choose to target your message, the more you are required to understand your ideal customer's likes and interests. We'll look at effectively profiling your audience in the next section, and how to tap into existing pools of potential customers through Like and Interest targeting.

Social Media Goal 4. Expose yourself to a new audience

If your business has traditionally been selling to one type of customer and you wish to transition to a new demographic or add different niches to your customer market, Social Media can help. We'll look at promoting your message in more detail elsewhere in this book, but identifying a leading figure in a new market, piggybacking their authority and using them to promote you can be extremely profitable. Not only do you get the credibility and endorsement, but you'll also pick up a number of 'curiosity clicks'. Using a respected celebrity this way ('celebrity' doesn't necessarily mean Hollywood red carpet, but a well-known figure amongst a certain group of people) can give your message an immediate elevation and position you in a new market very quickly.

Let's take a very small scale local example: a city pub situated close to a university has typically been frequented by a small regular group middle aged men having a drink after, and sometimes *instead of* work. Weekday nights are quiet though, and the pub owner envies the student traffic that their competitors seem to attract effortlessly. Finally he decides to do something about it and try to attract a younger student crowd on these nights to give them a more profitable mid week boost.

So he takes to social media, sets up an account and begin promoting some new deals on the types of drinks that young people buy. But because the pub doesn't have any student followers, these messages die like seeds sown in the desert. This is the point where most give up with social media, but not this pub owner. He takes a step back and identifies a number of online 'celebrities' amongst the nearby student population: heads of University societies, organisers of University socials, student events accounts and so on. All these people have a large social media following and high credibility amongst the sort of ideal customers they want to attract (students). The pub then creates extremely targeted promotions for each of these celebrity figures, for example special offers on drinks for members of a particular society after their fortnightly meet up. By targeting a narrow niche and creating a specific offer, they stand much more chance of having their offer shared with the society members, who are then more likely to convert into customers. The society social secretary feels important for being singled out by the pub, the society members get a deal on their drinks and the pub gets students through the door.

Who does your audience admire, and how could you piggyback on their profile to appear in front of more potential customers? Who would you ask to come and speak at a conference held for your customers?

Social Media Goal 5. Encourage repeat business

Much of the hype around Social Media is to do with attracting new customers, and the opportunity is no doubt huge. But what many fail to recognise is the potential to boost engagement and repeat purchases with *existing* customers. Successful social media campaigns will often encourage their customers to like and follow them to get special exclusive deals and offers only available to their followers. Once a customer sat waiting to pay the bill at a restaurant has decided to log on and follow that restuarant on Twitter, they are a part of the herd. If their attention is used in a respectful way, they'll be receptive to tweets about special offers, dishes of the day, seasonal specials and so on - all messages that they would otherwise never have received, leading to repeat business that might have otherwise never happened.

The effect of driving repeat business this way should not be underestimated. Remember that if a customer chooses to like or follow a restaurant, there's a fairly good chance that they have had a good experience. The sales job required to get this customer back to the restaurant for another visit is much simpler (and cheaper) than the sales job required to get a *new* customer in for the first time - but it still needs to be done. Keeping in your past customers' news feeds, and therefore their minds, in the future means that they won't forget about you.

All this restaurant owner now needs is for the circumstances to be right: perhaps the prospect is in the area on the way home from work, hungry and there's nothing in the fridge. They check Twitter on the bus, see that the restaurant is offering a one-night only deal of 3 courses for £19.00 and decide to make an impulse purchase. If the restaurant is really smart, they allow the hungry worker to reserve a table by tweeting them so all their friends can see, driving referral business as well. This leads us nicely on to...

Social Media Goal 6. Generate referrals

Once someone has bought from you they have the potential to become an extremely effective walking, talking, tweeting advertisement. But very few people will do this out of their own initiative. Encouraging referral business on social media is often played with, but not very creatively.

Referral solicitations on social media usually starts and ends with "Retweet to be in with a chance of winning a $100 voucher" or something equally uninspiring. Campaigns like this are dull and imaginative, and the response rates reflect this (although it's important to say that dull and imaginative is still better than nothing at all!).

Turbocharge your social media referral generation by understanding a few important principles:

1. Each of your followers is considered an authority by *their* followers. Recommendations they make are more significant therefore because of who is making them.
2. People Retweet and Share things for a number of reasons, but very rarely through wanting to help you out or simply 'spread the word'. Whether it's to appear as an insider with access to exclusive information, to get a real reward (discount, gift or voucher) or because their association with you boosts their own self image, it's important to understand which of these approaches you are trying to tap into. Reward referrers with attractive vouchers, free gifts and special offers; make offers exclusive to social media to excite the 'insider' feeling and give your sharers the sense that they are on the 'inside'. Remember that everybody acts from a place of

self interest, so there has to be something in it for them, even if it's a feeling of significance.

3. Many markets contain tastemakers - authorities on all that is new and good. People who see themselves as tastemakers will seek out and promote causes, organisations and businesses that they feel match their criteria and enhance their position by sharing. Going back to the restaurant example above, each town has its 'foodies' who like the feeling of discovering and championing a new great place to eat. They love the thrill of being the first to know about a new restaurant and one of the first to share their knowledge with their followers. Rather than doing this purely from a 'spreading the word' standpoint, they are doing this to increase their positioning as a tastemaker and source of knowledge. If a tastemaker has enough authority, their approval can be a huge boost to the visibility and exposure of your business. Like fitness clothing companies sending merchandise to influential fitness bloggers on Instagram and Pinterest, there is likely to be *something* you can do to attract the attention and goodwill of these tastemakers. It's important to understand the mindset of the tastemaker though, and allow them the feeling of 'discovering' you - by all means send free stuff, but don't pitch it too hard or they'll feel like you are trying to control them, and that's like Kryptonite to someone who has

built up their own brand by providing trustworthy personal recommendations.

Social Media Goal 7. Give your business a personality in an otherwise bland market

This is for the maker of air conditioning fans, the medical device manufacturer or the plumbers' merchant who is thinking "well this is all OK for companies selling 'cool' consumer-focussed products, but what about me?"

The good news is that whatever you sell, your customers are still human beings. If your market is the most boring, commoditized and <u>dull</u> market in the world, you're not going to be the only person thinking this. Your buyers still use social media. Perhaps not for business, but some will still be on Twitter, Facebook, Instagram or Pinterest in their spare time, and while the boss isn't looking at work. If you can be the first company to inject some personality into your market and give your audience something that will actually interest them, then you'll be the king in the land of the blind.

In a purely commoditized industry, price rules. If there are absolutely no distinguishing features of your product or service (see Social Media Goal 2) and you truly are selling a commodity, you can inject some personality to build familiarity and personality where none previously existed. This is now your differentiator. Given the choice between purchasing from two identical companies - one who is essentially unknown and one who has been building familiarity through their social media personality, sharing interesting industry-related content and even some off-topic entertainment, and who answers customer service queries through Twitter and Facebook, who would you choose?

The important takeaway is to understand your audience: their interests, problems and even hopes and dreams. If you can portray a social media personality that appeals to them, then all of a sudden you are not 'just another option' but the most familiar and trustworthy option.

So those are a summary of the most profitable social media goals. It's likely that some will resonate more than others and that's OK. Identifying your own unique mix of the above gives you a solid foundation to begin shaping the message of your profitable social media campaign.

How to Craft Your Social Media Message

Once you have your goal (or goals) in mind, it's time to create a message for your communications. Just like the goal it's important to specify your message clearly, because the more clearly your message is defined to yourself and your organisation, the more likely it is to come through in all your communications.

Businesses who have a clear online message tend to receive more followers. A definite personality behind the brand, even if it's not tied to a particular person, helps make it seem more human. And that's far more engaging to people than an inconsistent or mixed message.

This clarity of message is easiest to see at the extremities: really cheap companies who adopt a somewhat confrontational 'us against the world in our crusade for low prices' stance, and luxury brands that take an 'only the finest will do' stance. Each of these has its place and will appeal to a certain type of customer. Low budget customers who perceive the world in a grand conspiracy to rip them off and exploit them will identify with a budget airline crusading against anyone trying to increase charges against their customers, whether it's a government increasing fuel taxes or an entire country increasing air taxes. Meanwhile high end customers might appreciate the smug confidence of Gucci's profile which doesn't talk about anything other than the brand and how fantastic their products are. Almost 800,000 twitter followers don't seem to mind reading about this every day because that's what they expect from Gucci. It's a message consistent with the brand, despite being a lot more focussed on themselves and their brand than most companies can get away with on social media. What they understand is that their followers follow in order to buy into and experience the Gucci world. The value to their audience comes from association with Gucci as opposed to Gucci's sharing of relevant and useful information. Gucci wouldn't mock their competitors or tweet cat jokes, yet for a different business altogether these sort of strategies would work much more effectively than constantly talking about their own products..

Your social media message doesn't have to be as extreme as this, but elements from examples like these can be adopted and adapted to suit your audience. Overall, it is important that you decide your angle in advance and try to stick to it.

Often a brand's social media personality follows that of the business owner (think Virgin for example). So if that's you, what do you stand for and against? What's the personality you want your audience to attribute to your business? This can be a good starting point for your company's voice.

A consistent personality throughout your social media builds a sense of trust and familiarity in your audience. It's this which, over time, will give you a competitive edge when they come to choose between you and your competitors. This is worth spending some time on and is the sort of thing some brands take many years to finetune so don't feel a pressure to get it 100% right immediately.

Exercise - Creating Your Social Media Personality

In this exercise, we're going to walk through the process of creating your social media personality. There are a list of questions below that you can use to start to identify what sets you apart and what makes you different in your industry. These elements will form the basis of your message.

1. If you started your business yourself, why? What was it about the market that convinced you there needed to be another provider?
2. If you inherited the business, what about it appealed to you?
3. Why do customers choose you? Why *should* they? What's the real difference between you and your competitors? How do you communicate this to your customers and what's in it for them?
4. Do you have a greater level of expertise than your competitors? If so, how can you show your audience?
5. What do customers hate about your industry? How can you align with this and present a compelling alternative?
6. What do customers say when they walk into your shop, talk to your team or receive your product or service for the first time?
7. If your business was a film character, who would they be and why? Who would your main competitor be?

8. Which of your character traits most appeal to your audience?

If this is new thinking, answering these questions might not be easy. It's important not just to focus on the ones which you can answer quickly, because it's usually the questions we don't know the answers to that provide us with new insights.

The outcome of the exercise might be that you decide to let your own personality shine through your company's social media to a greater extent. That's a worthy result. The most important thing is to keep the personality consistent through all social media interactions so your customers can feel a sense of familiarity with your business.

Understanding your target customer

As mentioned previously, if you are crafting a message intended to appeal to your target customer, you'll obviously need to be extremely familiar with their likes, dislikes and even hopes and dreams. Knowing what they stand for and against means you can align your social media personality with them, building rapport.

While you might have a few different types of target customer it's likely that they will all have something in common. And it's this which is what draws them to you. Perhaps it's their appreciation of being treated like an individual, their taste for quality, or their love of a bargain. This should become the basis of your core message.

Narrow Niche Customer Targeting

For some businesses, their target customer fits into a relatively narrow profile. This means that their message can be precisely tuned to appeal to this group, and focussed on motivating the desired outcome (awareness, making a sale directly or branding/positioning). In many ways this niche targeting is made easier precisely because the message can be so narrow.

If we take a look at 3 examples of businesses that play in the sportswear retail market we can see how each has identified a particular type of customer that makes up their core audience, and how their message is tuned so specifically to that audience that engagement levels are extremely high. The 3 businesses vary from very narrow niche to a much broader market, giving us a glimpse at the different approaches used with varying customer types.

JD Sports, Sports Direct and Sweaty Betty all sell clothing and accessories for sports, yet their target audiences are quite different. At the time of writing, all 3 are advertising 'SALE' using their Twitter cover photos, but how this comes across in their streams is interesting. Their social media communications are so in tune with their core brand message, that most people familiar with the 3 companies would have no trouble attributing messages taken from any of them to the correct source. Generic social media this is not.

JD Sports (@JDSportsFashion) understands that their audience is not the bargain basement, price-driven customer but those who want the latest, newest and trendiest sportswear. Their feed reflects this as they share new hot of the press products, background information and pictures. As their twitter handle suggests, a large portion of their market isn't particularly driven by sports *performance* but rather sports *fashion* (although it's important from a positioning standpoint that customers believe that the merchandise is the latest and most up-to-date in performance and technology as well, even if it is never used in a sports environment). This approach works well when sales are the goal, but JD Sports are never particularly 'salesy'. They avoid publishing Buy it Now links and with strong calls to action, for example, trusting that their customers know where to go if they want to buy the products. The purpose of the Twitter account then is to collect an audience who is passionate about the latest in sportswear fashion and associate the JD Sports brand with this.

Meanwhile Sports Direct caters to a much wider market united by one common thread: price. They use a permanent 'All stock must go' heavily-discounted angle to attract a wide variety of price-driven customers, whether or not these customers are into sport. Similar to the McDonalds example covered later, their customer profile is too wide to make a specific product-driven strategy particularly effective, so instead they take a more general approach focusing on sporting events, weather and cheering for UK athletes. Because of the variation in their audience interests, they can't really target specific products or even focus too heavily on individual sports for fear of alienating large parts of their audience. The result is more of a standard awareness campaign intended to boost the visibility of Sports Direct in their customers' daily lives, whilst also giving the brand a personality that price-driven retailers can often lack.

Sweaty Betty's target audience on the other hand is much narrower; specifically affluent women who are into fitness. Their customers aren't price driven and are more interested in looking good and the feeling of exclusivity from buying a higher-end brand. Because their audience tends to match a particular profile, they are able to focus on specific product-promotion, information on fitness trends (as long as they are relevant to the types of exercise their audience does) and retweeting & promotion of articles mentioning Sweaty Betty. It's an example of a positioning and alignment approach ("we are all women into fitness just like you") whilst they also seek to add value with content likely to be of interest to their audience.

So here we see three companies all selling sports clothing but who have identified clearly who their audience is and use their social media profiles to grow their herd. For many businesses, the difference between profitable and unprofitable social media is understanding your audience and crafting a message engaging enough to keep them interested long enough for that awareness and familiarity to influence a purchase. In that sense, companies with a narrow audience like Sweaty Betty and JD Sports are at an advantage, because audience targeting is easier for them than for a price or convenience-driven business with a wider audience.

Wide Customer Targeting

An example of a business whose target customer is spread across numerous demographic and interest groups is McDonalds. From businessmen and women picking up a coffee on the way to work, teenagers grabbing lunch before heading to the movies and parents taking their children for a hassle-free dinner, McDonalds' audience doesn't sit in one specific category. So what do these distinct groups all have in common? How can Ronald and all those spotty teenagers engage everyone through social media without alienating at least some of their audience? What sort of topics can be universal in their appeal but still give McD a chance to build a brand persona?

Taking a look at the official US McDonalds (@McDonalds) twitter feed gives us some clues: music, love of the weekend, patriotism and (at the time of writing) celebration of summer weather. These threads are found in almost all McDonalds tweets, leaving no one feeling left out or unable to identify with the social media message. The other common thread running through their communications is charity, although this more for positioning benefits than to identify with a particular audience group. Sure, it's not the sort of highly-targeted message that is going to drive a lot of sales, but by being inoffensive and staying present in their audience's newsfeed, they have captive eyeballs and a small piece of daily 'mindshare'.

Arguably McDonalds could run specific promotion-driven campaigns for new products and special offers, but here they run into yet another dilemma for large companies using social media: a worldwide audience. While US customers might respond well to the latest variation on a cheeseburger for $5.99, customers in other countries who are clearly unable to participate will be left feeling disengaged. To make matters worse, even within the US there are region-specific offers and pricing variations. This makes an offers-based strategy more challenging and really limits the scope of the social media message.

Taking all of the above into consideration, it's no surprise that the McD twitter strategy is based around being an extension of the brand and giving a friendly, 'real life' personality to the company.

What to do if your target audience doesn't use Social Media

Some businesses will assume that their core audience doesn't use social media. Even if this is true (which it often isn't. Usually the buyers in even the most boring industries use *some* social media, if not for work) it doesn't necessarily mean that it can't be a profitable use of time and energy.

As well as the SEO benefits (which we discuss in another chapter), there are networking opportunities open to businesses wanted to establish new profitable relationships with others in their industry. One of our clients is a luxury home technology company whose clients are often wealthy foreign businessmen with homes in the UK. This sort of customer isn't going to be tweeting them questions about home automation wiring any time soon.

In fact most of their customers aren't involved in the buying decisions at all. But by providing an up-to-date and aspirational social media profile covering the latest in home technology and interiors, they can attract an audience of interior design companies and other businesses involved in high end home renovation. Following, retweeting and interacting with these potential business partners and sources of referrals means they can be actively involved in a sort of online community whilst building their profile and making potentially profitable connections.

So if your reaction is that your audience doesn't use social media, a) check that assumption and b) find an audience that *does* and can still make you money from.

Fine Tuning Your Message Over Time
As you begin marketing using social media, it's important not to stress about getting it 100% right first time. You might find that your audience is unlike what you expected, and therefore you need to slightly adjust your core message. You might find that your audience varies by social network as well. Over time you'll learn what sort of content really appeals to your fans, followers and friends, and how you can structure any promotions you run to maximise engagement.

But rather than spending too long worrying and asking the 'What if?' questions, the important thing is just to *start.* If you're active and willing to experiment, you will find an approach that works for you and gives you the results that you're after. Accept that it's not going to be perfect right off the bat, keep your eyes open and be receptive to feedback about how well your campaign is being received.

Choosing Your Method

So far we have thought about our **M**essage, which is designed to appeal to our audience, reflect our brand's core values and celebrate what makes us different. We then sought to understand our **M**arket, helping us to hone and focus this message to have the biggest impact amongst our audience.

The third step is choosing your **M**ethod of communication. We'll be looking at getting to grips with each of the social channels in the next section of the book, but for now it's important to start thinking about where your audience is most likely to spend time online so you can meet them where they already hang out. As we'll see, each audience has it's preferred networks and what might work well for a brand on Twitter could do nothing for the same brand if applied to Pinterest for example.

Figures from the Pew Research Centre's Internet & American Life study from November 2012 gives us some interesting stats on relative Social Media popularity and demographic. Facebook was found, unsurprisingly, to be the network used by the largest total number of internet users (67%), with Twitter, Pinterest and Instagram at 16%, 15% and 13% respectively. Where the results start to get more interesting is in the gender splits: 72% of women internet users use social media compared to 62% of men. Twitter is slightly more popular amongst men, but image-based Instagram and Pinterest are more popular with women - particularly Pinterest, which women are 5 times more likely to use than men. The research also shows that as household income rises, so does Pinterest use, matching the experience of many in the Internet Marketing world who have seen high-end female-oriented products sell particularly well as a result of Pinterest sharing.

But these stats and our experience are intended to be guidelines only. Social Media is still relatively new and patterns such as the above are still in a state of flux as different niches discover uses for each of the social networks. There needs to be enough content creators on a network before a new audience group will be interested enough to commit time and energy to consuming it, so it's worth testing every relevant network to see how your potential audience responds. Even if you don't get the response *volume* you were hoping for, if the response *quality* is good then it can be worth sticking at it and waiting for the rest of your audience to join the party.

Remember to claim your free online marketing audit, if you haven't done so already, at www.exposureninja.com/audit

One of our expert social media team will send you free personal recommendations, competitor analysis and suggestions to grow your audience.

Creating a Following

In this section we'll be looking at a number of strategies that we can use to grow our following and boost our profile. Your goal for your social media campaign should not be quantity-driven ("I want to have 3,000 followers by June"), but rather driven by what we call *profitable influence*. Profitable influence is different to regular influence because - surprise surprise - it focuses on attracting more business for you through acquiring new customers and selling more to existing customers.

Rather than aim purely for volume then, a profitable social media campaign will raise your profile *amongst people who can give you money or have access to others who can give you money*. Everything else is just a pleasant but unnecessary ego boost. The ideal result is that when buyers of your product or service are in the moment of need, you are there at the front of their mind. This doesn't happen overnight and it takes time.

Let's think of some real world examples:

You're looking for a dentist in your area to book in the family for a check up. You Google "dentists" and open a few tabs. One of the dentists mentions that people who Like their Facebook page get free teeth whitening with every dental treatment. There's a button to Like the page right underneath the offer with a call to action that says "Like us Now for your Free Teeth Whitening", so you click it. While you're clicking around the other dentists in your area, you decide that actually you're going to go for another dentist because they look cheaper and are slightly closer.

You book in and pay this competitor a visit, but you're not overly impressed - they tried to sell you expensive treatments you didn't think you needed and the office was tatty. You decide that you're probably not likely to go back, but for the time being your itch was scratched and you won't need to find a new dentist until your next checkup.

Meanwhile, your Facebook 'Like' on the other dentist's page still stands. Luckily for them, they've read lots of great social media books and they're providing lots of genuinely useful content on their page which appeals to potential customers, not just those who need a dentist right now. This social savvy dentist posts blogs on their website about things like "The most common tooth brushing mistake - are you inadvertently damaging your teeth twice per day?", "Is tooth whitening dangerous? How to get white teeth without causing long-term damage", "How to teach your kids how to brush their teeth" and "How to choose the best toothbrush (TIP: the most expensive ones are NOT the best!)" - things that ordinary people would find interesting and that would get them thinking about their teeth.

This dentist doesn't go crazy promoting blog posts 3 times a day, because people just don't *need* that much tooth information in their lives; always remember that 'unlike' is just a click away for people who feel they're being subjected to excessive advertising.

But over the course of a year let's say we see 15 articles of real interest posted by this dentist and we click on and read 5 - just 30% - of these. That means we've been to their site 5 times and are familiar with them, their personality, and the business. This puts them miles ahead of the other dentists in our town, who remain completely anonymous.

When it comes time to book that next check up, one of two things will happen:
1. We enquire with the Facebook dentist first, as we're already familiar and have built a small amount of rapport with them.
2. We'll search "dentist" again, ask a friend for a recommendation, or embark on any other dentist-finding operation. During the course of this research phase, we're drawn to mentions of the Facebook dentist. We recognise their name, we feel safe with them and we remember that we've got that free tooth whitening treatment with our first appointment.

Either way, that dentist's social media activity has just greatly increased their chances of making a sale. If they can deliver a great experience, then this social campaign is also going to boost repeat business as they stick in our minds and continue to build rapport between appointments as well.

Over a number of years, that dentist becomes a real part of our consciousness and gets access to our attention *infinitely more* than her competitors, who are invisible in our day to day life. This dentist doesn't have to be better, cheaper or more convenient - those things are totally irrelevant. Their competitive advantage is *familiarity and rapport*. And in a world where few businesses have any competitive advantage at all, that's enough!

In this way, social media allows you to boost your profile amongst your target audience no matter how high-profile you are by other metrics. If you scan through your own Facebook timeline, Twitter or G+ feed you'll notice that there are businesses, seminar speakers and other entities that are really a part of your *daily* or even *hourly* consciousness due to their intelligent use of social media. They're probably not the most famous businesses, speakers and others that you know of, and they're probably not the *best*, but they're the ones you remember and are familiar with. This point cannot be understated, as it sums up effective social media strategy in one paragraph.

Using Implied Association to Build Your Profile

Never have we had such easy access to the thought-leaders in our fields. They're just an @reply away, and everybody can see that communication in public. Those who claim social media is a fad are failing to understand the strange human attraction to celebrities*. And the thing that most people want from celebrities above anything else? *Access*. If they can get this access from social media, they'll continue to be hooked.

*'Celebrities' in this context is used to describe high profile figures in any industry. They don't have to be a household name as long as they're recognised by their peers and audience as having significant influence.

Deeper than this, social media allows associations to be built (or implied - there's very little difference in the minds of your audience) more easily than ever before. Of course, nothing will replace real solid personal relationships involving handshakes and lunches, but for those of us who are too busy *doing* to be out schmoozing, social can give us a handy shortcut when we want to 'borrow' authority from established figures.

A plain Retweet can be a significant implied endorsement. It says to the authority's followers: "this person says what I'm thinking so I don't even need to comment". If that authority figure is in your industry or market, a retweet like this can generate a decent boost in follower numbers and significantly elevate your position in the minds of the clan. Keep reading to find out how to attract this sort of retweet.

A conversation with an authority figure can do the same. Providing the conversation is natural and reasonably equal, it can raise your profile amongst both your followers and the followers of the authority, whether or not they are already familiar with you.

Getting High Profile Retweets and Starting Conversations

So how do you go about getting retweeted or starting a conversation with an authority figure in your industry?

The important thing to remember is that your target 'celebrity' is in a place of authority for a reason: because they understand **power**. They know how to appear powerful and they understand (sometimes unconsciously) how to give their ideas and opinions the sort of weight that makes them seem more significant.

Just like anybody else, the question running through their heads the whole time is "What's in it for me?" There has to be a clear benefit to them if they are going to share your post or reply to you. On social media, this clear benefit is usually a feeling of *significance*. Anything they RT or reply to is usually something that strengthens their position of power or authority. This could be validation of a principle or idea that they are known for promoting; it could be recognition of their impact; it could be a piece of news that would give them significance for promoting to their followers.

He's completely self obsessed! (Just like me)
I'm not trying to paint these authorities as power-hungry, self obsessed *monsters* - they might be power-hungry self-obsessed *angels*. But the common thread between

people who strive to be high-profile is, yes, a certain hunger for power and a dash of self-obsession. This is somewhat inevitable: most humans only see one perspective (our own) and we all have this built in drive to elevate our social standing and be seen by others as more significant. That's why society holds together, and social media is a fantastic study on this behaviour. So rather than pretend self obsession and hunger for power doesn't exist, let's *use* it.

OK Back to the Story...
Your target retweeter then, is most likely to promote you if you present a message that they agree with, that reinforces their own stance on a certain topic, or appears to validate their position as an authority.

Getting them to actually see your message is as simple as including their Twitter handle at the end of your tweet and making sure you send it at a time of day when they are most active. You can look back through their history to see patterns of activity and notice when they tend to be most responsive. It's worth bearing in mind that they could be using automatic post scheduling software, in which case try to analyse the times of day that they are having conversations with followers rather than just tweeting. If they are active on twitter late at night, then this could be a great time to get their attention. If they're an early riser and you've noticed they tweet early, it could be that they tweet over breakfast (or from bed!) so make sure your message is right there in front of them. If they're really high profile, they might be getting a constant flood of @replies, in which case you're certainly going to have to be strategic with your timing in order to get noticed.

An important consideration when trying to get a response from someone high profile is that you don't damage your own positioning in the process. If your followers see your outreach attempts as desperate or they make you come across as needy, this could alter your followers' perception of you. Here are some tips to avoid this:

- Don't be desperate or suck up in your message. Saying someone *reminded* you of an important principle or idea gives you more implied power than getting all gushy thanking someone for helping you see the light for the first time. Be respectful, but also remember that if you want to be treated like an authority, *you must first act like someone with authority*.
- If you want to limit the visibility of your outreach attempts, using an @reply at the start of your tweet will hide the tweet from people's feeds who aren't following your target.
- If they don't respond, don't keep harassing them. If your profile looks like a constant stream of unreturned outreach attempts, what does that say about you? Desperation is the least attractive behaviour in marketing.
- Similarly, go easy on the volume of your outreach and don't forget the goal of your social media campaign in the first place. You want to

be the guru in the mind of your audience, and what sort of guru leaves their flock alone while they go chasing lots of other gurus all day long trying to get endorsement? A RT or conversation outreach every so often is fine, but too much makes you appear desperate and raises questions over your own authority status.

Key questions to ask then are: Who are the authority figures in your industry? What sort of content do they share, and how could you reach out to them for implied endorsement?

Creating 'Shareworthy' Content

Creating particularly shareworthy content requires some thought and, yes, a little hard work. Spur of the moment offers ("10% off" - boring!) or updates about your business ("new website!" - who cares?) just aren't going to cut it.

Here are some content creation strategies to boost your social sharing and raise your authority. Some are easy, some require more effort; some are cheap, some involve an investment. Rather than head straight for the easy ones (that's what everyone else will do), seriously consider the ones that make you uncomfortable or stretch you outside your comfort zone:

- Run an industry survey. This doesn't have to be any more complicated than setting up a questionnaire in Google Drive (free) and surveying your audience, customers or industry peers. If your questions are geared towards generating insights that aren't commonly known, or you are able to quantify a pattern or trend that you see developing, the results of this survey could be very interesting to your market. Publish them on your website first, then link to them from your social media updates and notify everyone who participated in the survey. You can also contact prominent relevant publications and news outlets - you'd be amazed at how easy it is to get some press coverage with a good survey. When trying to get attention, it helps if you can pick out a shocking, surprising or otherwise eye catching stat to use as a headline for the survey as this can be used to attract attention and stop people in their tracks.

- Review products or services that are relevant to your audience. Give plenty of detail and include other media (pictures, videos etc) where possible to make the review as valuable and comprehensive as possible. Again if you can find a headline in there ("Has X Just Rendered All Other Ys Obsolete?" or "X Stuns the ABC Industry with a revolutionary take on Z") then you are more likely to attract the attention of the people you need. Again, once the review is live on your site, share it on social media and promote the review to anyone who will listen, including the business behind the reviewed product.

- Give future predictions, remarking on a certain aspect close to the hearts of others in your industry, again thinking about an eye catching headline: "The Game Changer for Small Businesses: How small business online marketing just changed forever and what you need to do immediately to survive". I defy any small business owner's interest NOT to be peaked there...
- Interview leading figures about the future of your industry. Publish the interview on your website, then post it out on social media tagging the industry figure involved. If they're like most people, they'll then retweet this as it boosts their credibility in the eyes of their audience. As always if you can include a catchy or controversial headline, other people are more likely to be interested and as a result retweet it.

The rules with creating new original content for social media are:

1. Publish it on your website first. If it generates a lot of shares, you want to make sure these links are pointing at *your* site rather than anyone else's. The only exception is when you are writing for a high-profile publication, and using this for credibility.
2. Good headlines generate clicks. "7 Ways to..." "Five quick tips for successful..." "The shocking truth about..." If you're thinking that this all sounds a bit sensationalist, then you're right, but

that stuff works. Of course you and I are much too sophisticated to fall prey to such obvious headlines as these, right? Any serious marketing student can do worse than study the headlines on tabloid newspaper websites.

3. Include a brief summary at the start of a longer piece so people interested can bookmark for later, or share without reading the whole thing. Remember that people use social media to fill spare *minutes* not hours so making your content easy to digest is important. This isn't to say it should lack substance, but you should aim to give people with only 1-2 minutes enough value to make them want to return later.

4. Make sure your website is responsive (meaning that it looks good on mobile). Content on responsive websites tends to do better because people can read it on their phones whilst they watch their child's school play, spend intimate time with a loved one or navigate the busy rush hour traffic.

5. If you can tie in a current event or celebrity, people's radars will already be tuned to receive your message. As a great recent example, take a look at the number of hair transplant articles that mention English footballer Wayne Rooney to see how you can piggyback on celebrity news for maximum exposure. Most of the clinics using him in their stories had no affiliation to him whatsoever, but recognised that even just

mentioning him implied endorsement and made it more likely their content would be shared.

Using Controversy

Controversy is a great way to become active and engaged in your market, particularly if you are offering a new way of doing things, or you want to be perceived that way.

If you know that your customers have a particular gripe or distaste for how things are done in your industry, siding with them to stand against the established players can build affinity and trust which, as well as boosting your social media visibility, can earn you business directly.

As an example, I've come to hate most SEO companies who aren't transparent about the strategies they are using and, by continuing to do what they *used to do* to promote websites in 2009, are getting their innocent clients penalised. The good news is that most of the world's SEO clients also hate this lack of transparency (and they also hate getting penalties). So by arming them with the knowledge and strategies to fight this 'enemy' of other SEO companies, we can show how we're different and position ourselves in a way that makes us stand out.

If we were in a position to need more clients (at the time of writing we have around 200 unanswered leads, so we definitely do NOT need more clients!), I would have absolutely no hesitation to start calling out the particular guilty SEO companies responsible over social media. If I am happy to wave my arms around and kick up enough of a fuss, this 'war' will be played out in public and generate publicity Exposure Ninja, and me as the figurehead. Press releases about the argument can be prepared and sent to relevant industry magazines and blogs, generating even more publicity. If the enemy is smart, they'll play along because they'll *also* be generating publicity for themselves. With good damage limitation and smart strategy even the 'victim' in these sorts of stunts can quite easily come out of the other side with their reputation unscathed but profile raised.

If you look at Donald Trump's very public 'war' with Rosie O'Donnell (timed carefully to coincide with the the new series of The Apprentice), both parties benefitted from a profile boost and saw their TV and print exposure increase as a result. Stories about the feud spread over social media and continue to do so every time either of them needs a bit of publicity. While this is a high profile example, the underlying principles exist at any scale.

In my opinion the ultimate master of courting controversy to boost their own profile and grow their business is @KimDotcom, the founder of Megaupload and it's new incarnation Mega. His services are used by Internet users around the world, but his primary and most profitable target audience could (perhaps controversially) be identified as those who upload and download pirated software, games, media and other files using his sites. Kim is absolutely magnetic to this market with his unique mixture of part underdog, part pirate, part obnoxiously rich troublemaker. He's all too happy to speak out publicly against any establishment from the US government to Hollywood rights holders, and a good dose of his outrageous 'you can't catch me' personality makes for extremely entertaining viewing.

Managing to strike this fine balance between power (his Megaupload site was estimated to be responsible for 4% of all internet traffic at its peak) and victimisation (he lives in New Zealand and is constantly fighting extradition attempts), his audience regards him as somewhat godlike. By constantly courting controversy and being so outspoken, each of his new online businesses generates a phenomenal amount of publicity and awareness without costing him a penny. It's a brilliant strategy that costs him nothing (aside from the legal fees his sites result in!).

Controversy without ruffling feathers

Some readers will feel uneasy at the idea of courting controversy because they're naturally averse to confrontation. But it's worth bearing in mind that not all controversy is created equal, and not all requires confrontation. Much like Orwell's Two Minutes Hate, a lot of apparent controversy can be generated by picking a fight against an enemy that can't or won't fight back - or even that doesn't exist. This strategy can also be summed up as 'finding a parade to stand in front of'.

If we take a look at the semi-recent outpouring of emotion against SOPA (the Stop Online Piracy Act) which resulted in online protests from thousands of websites and millions of web users, the object of this mammoth focus of public hate was US legislators. It became clear quite early on that online public support was heavily in favour of blocking SOPA, and that the legislators weren't going to launch a meaningful resistance. By choosing an enemy like this to 'campaign' against, many savvy social media users used the STOP SOPA movement to raise their own profile and build perceived authority. They stood in front of an existing parade against an enemy that refused to defend itself.

Every industry has a common enemy in some shape, whether it's the 'old guard', legislation, trends or fashions, snobbery, elitism, vulgarity or ignorance. If you're stuck for ideas, ask yourself 'what would you end up bitching about if you and your ideal customer started drinking together?'

By positioning yourself against this enemy you can tap into the conversation your audience is already having in their heads, and encourage sharing as people retweet your message to emphasise and give validity to their own feelings.

Hashtags and Entering Existing Conversations

Originating on Twitter, hashtags are a way that an audience can categorise or 'tag' their posts by a certain theme. When people are interested in a certain hashtag - for example if they are following a particular event - they might search for other tweets using that hashtag to see what other people are saying about it. By tagging your posts with this hashtag, you can appear in front of this highly relevant audience.

Many industry conferences will have a publicised hashtag that visitors can use to discuss the speakers, topics and anything else relating to the event. If you can add value or provide insight during these conferences that other delegates would find interesting, you'll be able to pick up some extra targeted followers.

If these event attendees are potential customers, you can publicise a special offer for delegates using a hashtag and collects some really good quality leads that you can follow up after the conference. For example:

"Free #socialmedia audits for visitors to the #exposureninjaconference2014 Retweet this message then click here: exposureninja.com/audit"

This takes no time to set up, is completely free and can generate a good level of interest if the offer matches the audience well.

The Social Networks

Now we're taken a look at some of the strategy and planning behind a profitable social media campaign, let's dive a little deeper into each of the social networks and take a look at some specific techniques, intricacies and quirks relevant to each.

Facebook

Here's a fun fact about Facebook marketing: according to HubSpot, about 41% of B2B companies have generated a customer with Facebook. This demonstrates how useful a tool Facebook is for marketing your business, even in a B2B market. Remember that whether you're B2B or B2C, your target customer is still a human being, and it's increasingly likely that this human being is using Facebook not only to connect with other human beings but also brands and companies they identify with. It can be a great source of leads and customers, but even regular *personal* users can find it difficult at first to figure out how exactly to use Facebook to benefit their *business*. With the right knowledge and metrics however, those leads are just a few clicks away.

Before getting started with Facebook marketing it is important that you set some smart goals:

1. Get Found: It is important that your business page is easily accessible and can be found on Facebook for the products and services that you provide. Including mentions of your key products, services and solutions in your description increases the chance that you'll show up in searches (both on Facebook and on Google), and communicating with other Facebook pages relevant to your industry can introduce you to new groups of people.

2. Engagement: To get your Facebook campaign off to a good start, connect and engage with your existing customers, stakeholders and potential future clients. By including links to your Facebook page on outgoing emails and on your website you'll start picking up existing customers as followers. But beware: the more followers you start to build, the more communication you will start to attract. This communication can't be ignored, and unless you build a process around this or commit regular time to responding, it can all too easily get left behind.

3. Community Building: As a business owner and/or marketer you understand how important it is to build a community of dedicated fans and followers around your brand. This takes time but stick with it, particularly while you're finding your stride and building your audience. Keeping your page active helps, as does providing useful content which helps your audience overcome important challenges in their lives or businesses.

4. Promotion of Content: Promoting your own content as well as content relevant to your business is important when it comes to social media marketing. This is an important part of a profitable Facebook campaign, but it is still only one part. When thinking about the balance between promoting your content and being genuinely interesting to your audience remember this: if there was no content between the adverts on TV, *nobody would watch TV*. So be sensitive to your audience's tolerance for advertising and don't forget to include plenty of value *first*, before sharing your message.

5. Leads and Sales: This is an important element of profitable social media marketing, but it shouldn't be beaten to death as nothing can drive an audience away like a never ending sales pitch clogging up their Newsfeed.

Setting Up Your Facebook Business Page

You can't create a Facebook Business Page without creating your own personal profile, so if you don't already have a personal profile that is the first step. Once you've setup your personal profile you can create a Facebook Business page here: http://www.facebook.com/pages/create/php. You will see 6 different page options:

1. Local business or page
2. Company, organization or institution
3. Brand or Product
4. Artist, Band or Public Figure
5. Entertainment
6. Cause or Community

Select the type of page that you want to create, choose the category your brand falls into and add your company name. Facebook will now help you get started by walking you through 3 steps: Selecting your profile picture, adding a small description of your business under the 'About' section and enabling ads.

When writing your business description don't forget your audience walking around with "what's in it for me?" playing in a loop inside their heads. <u>Your description isn't really a description of your business so much as a sentence or two about why your potential customers should do business with you</u>. Remember to always think benefits: what makes you different? Why are you better? What do your customers get from their relationships with you?

Once the page is created you can edit any of information about your page by clicking on the 'Edit Page' option on the Admin Panel. You can also permit a number of people to manage your page by clicking on the 'Manage Admin Roles' option and adding their profiles. You can assign roles such as 'Manager', 'Content Creator', 'Moderator', 'Advertiser', and 'Insights Analyst' which give different privileges, so you don't have to give the new girl the keys to the whole castle.

There are various options that you can choose, for example adding various apps to your page, managing who can or can't post on your page, adding a cover photo, longer descriptions and contact details. Contact details are particularly important from an SEO perspective as they form a valuable citation which can help boost your visibility in local searches, so if you're a business with a physical address this section is a must.

Your choice about who can post on your page really depends on your business, your audience size and the resources you have dedicated to managing this communication. If possible, you want to allow people to post on your page to encourage interaction, but for some businesses this won't be practical.

Your Cover Photo

Adding a cover photo is a good idea because it gives you an opportunity for instant engagement with your audience. Try to choose a cover photo that sums up your offering in one picture and that conveys the benefits of choosing you immediately. If you're fun and different, that's a good message to convey; if you're reliable and established, including pictures of your certifications and accreditations can help communicate this. A big picture of your logo with no indication of what you do or what makes you different is not 'optimal', however intuitive it might seem.

Your cover photo should measure at least 399 pixels wide, with the ideal dimensions being 851 x 315. It's also important to make sure that any text in your cover photo covers no more than 20% of the area, or you risk it being disapproved under Facebook's advertising guidelines.

Your Profile Picture

Most businesses will choose their logo as their profile picture, but it's important to make sure it's clearly recognisable. Wide but narrow logos can be difficult to read when shrunk down, as can those with a lot of words. Your logo should stand out in people's news feeds, so if your logo isn't easily readable as a profile photo you might consider having a square version made for use across your social media channels. If you need any help with this, do get in touch through the Exposure Ninja website.

Promoting Your Facebook Page and Attracting Likes

Rather than going overboard with promotional posts, the best way to promote your Facebook page is by simply sharing engaging content. Competition for your audience's news feed space is fierce and, as we'll see later on, the most engaging posts become more visible. It's also important to remember that anyone who doesn't like a particular post can immediately remove the post, or you, from their news feed forever. Once they're gone it's very difficult to get them back, so the best plan is not to lose them in the first place!

Post a variety of different content but make sure it is relevant to what your target audience is interested in. Keep things varied by mixing up your posts using photos, videos, status updates, events, polls, questions, greetings and articles. Asking your audience questions is a great way to engage them in a conversation with you and it will also make your posts more visible in more fans' news feeds, leading to visibility with people who do not know you yet.

As your page grows, your audience will start communicating with you more often. It's imperative that you respond to comments, questions, concerns posted on your page calmly, quickly and in a manner that reassures potential customers. Unanswered complaints is a huge turn off for new visitors, and although you might be tempted to ignore customer queries in the hope that they'll get the message and check your website for the answers, it gives the wrong impression if you're not seen to be responsive.

Whether people are complaining or complementing, acknowledge them and thank them for their feedback. And whatever you do, don't seek to prove people wrong - most people would rather kick up a fuss than admit they're wrong in public. While it can be frustrating that correspondence on social media seems to take priority over all else, it's the visibility that makes it so crucial to get right. And remember: do it all with a smile!

Quick Ninja Facebook Tips

1. One of the most attractive Facebook personas you can have is a mixture of fun and helpful.

Mentioning your products or services in passing or through the use of relevant and interesting testimonials and case studies is generally OK, but on the whole make sure that when people reach your page you provide them with entertainment and content that connects them with your brand. Keep a balance between entertainment and your serious side and don't be afraid to let your personality come through, it's *social* media after all.

2. Create anticipation. For the right businesses, your Facebook page can be a great way to get your audience excited and talk *to* you and *about* you. Offering them a sneak peek of your upcoming offers, discounts, new releases can create a feeling of exclusivity. To reward your fans for being a part of your Facebook community, consider if there's some sort of perk or 'treat' that you can offer them. This can breed a feeling of exclusivity as we've seen in some of the examples earlier in the book. Depending how playful they are, you can have your audience share your content, get you more likes, tag you in their status updates and various other engagement devices in return for something with perceived value or exclusivity.

3. Be the centre. The real-time nature of social media means it can be a good place for you to post the latest industry news. Make your page a place people turn to to be kept up-to-date about the latest goings on in your industry, as well as

entertain themselves. Becoming a thought leader like this takes work and a long-term commitment, but it can pay off in a big way once you've established yourself as an authority.

4. Boost credibility. Businesses that are active participants in their industry, communicating with other big players and with a lot of relevant high quality information benefit from a sense of credibility that other businesses with no social profile lack.

5. Engage. Yes, we know it's the most overused social media word in the English language, but there's a reason. Talk to people, interact, have fun and get out there. Don't be one of the boys at the school disco 'playing it cool' waiting for the girls to notice him, because the girls are too busy noticing the guy trying to dance, chatting to them and telling funny stories. Even if he's a terrible dancer, has nothing to talk about and is not particularly funny, people notice him. Over time the dancing will improve, the conversation will become more advanced and the stories will get funnier. So get out there and try out some Facebook moves. You heard it here first: social media is an extension of the school disco.

There's another reason why engagement is so important, and that's because it actually breeds more visibility...

Engagement - Facebook Edgerank Explained

Ever wondered why you see posts from some of your Facebook friends a lot more frequently than others? Noticed posts showing up in your feed from pages you've never heard from before? Wondered why you have hundreds of friends but only see posts from the same 25 on a daily basis? It's time to discuss Facebook 'Edgerank'...

Edgerank is, without a doubt, one of the most important algorithms when it comes to social media marketing. It determines which post appears on Facebook users' news feeds and which posts disappear without a trace. For anybody who wants to market their business on Facebook, understanding Edgerank can be the difference between being highly visible and being completely *in*visible.

So what is it and how can we manipulate it for our own evil gain?

First let's look at the word itself. The 'Edge' in Edgerank is the name Facebook gives to an action on the site. Each status update, photo post, comment, like, check-in etc is an Edge, and thus subject to Edgerank. The algorithm then decides how visible that Edge should be.

How? There are three factors that the Facebook Edgerank is based on: Affinity, Edge Weight and Time Decay. Let's look at them in turn:

Affinity: Affinity score is essentially a measure of your online social proximity to someone. Have you ever noticed how your newsfeed usually show you more updates from the people who you are in constant or recent contact with on Facebook rather than those you barely talk to? Have you 'stalked' someone's profile and then noticed that they have suddenly started showing up in your news feed regularly? Comment on someone's photos and see how they start to appear in your news feed all the time! You guessed it - this is affinity in action.

Using the vast amounts of data it collects, Facebook has detected that you are close with this person. The Edgerank algorithm has acknowledged this proximity and it has changed your news feed results accordingly.

Now an important note: Affinity is a one-way street. If you are visiting a friend's profile or a business page regularly, *you* are the only one who will be seeing more updates from that friend or page. It doesn't mean that *they* will start seeing more of *your* posts.

So how can you take advantage of Affinity to boost the profile of your business page?

If you are visiting another business page that is following you, this will not increase your Edgerank or visibility to them in any way. But if you comment on their updates and they comment back and/or visit your page in return, this *is* likely to increase your appearance on their newsfeed. So make sure to engage with other pages, your clients and potential clients in order to increase your Edgerank via your Affinity score. The more you engage with others and encourage them to engage with you, the higher your affinity and the higher your visibility.

Edge Weight: Edge weight is a formula that decides which Edges are more likely to appear in news feeds. Each type of Edge has a weighting factor, for example a status update is usually more interesting to your friends than if you like a business page; marriage notifications are generally more important than notifications about new friendships.

If you have already been doing some basic marketing on Facebook you'll have noticed that there are certain kinds of posts that seem to be weighted more heavily than others. Ever noticed how status updates seem to reach more people than the links that you post? Wondered why your Newsfeed tends to be full of pictures? Photos tend to be very heavily Edge-weighted, and you'll notice savvy social media marketers attach photos to their posts, links and status updates even if it's not necessary. They are doing this to increase the Edge weight and thus the chance of the post being seen, which in turn increases the chance of *interactions*, thus driving up the Edge weight even further, making the post still more visible. This sort of positive feedback loop is the reason behind the 'viral' behaviour of some posts.

There are two weight types: post and interactions. Once Edgerank has determined the *type* of Edge, the early interaction level will contribute to how much visibility the algorithm gives it.

So that's what Edge weight *is*, how can you take advantage of it to boost your business page?

The simplest way is rather than posting plain status updates, include a picture as well. Then, by posting at a time of day when you know your audience are most likely to be on Facebook, you can make sure you get maximum early interaction with your post, which in turn will boost its visibility further.

In addition you can aim to make your posts more interactive. Asking your audience questions, making controversial statements and sharing content which is likely to get a reaction from your audience will give your Edges more weight over time and you'll start to notice your posts having a wider reach.

It's well worth following Mashable, Techcrunch or one of the other technology blogs if you want to observe a company that truly understands Edgerank manipulation. You'll notice that most of their posts are designed to get a reaction one way or another from their audience, and as a result their updates are highly visible.

Ever wondered how those pages that share funny and amazing videos appear in your news feed so often, even if you don't like the page yourself? It's because they have such huge Edge weighting as a result of all the shares, likes and comments they generate that they appear in Newsfeeds of their fans' friends.

Of course this sort of shareability is difficult to create for any page that doesn't have huge mass appeal, but that doesn't mean it's impossible. It's certainly easier to make a video of a fat talking cat go viral than to get millions of shares for a letting agent's new property listing, but with some creativity even the most seemingly bland subject matter can be livened up a bit. With cats.

Time Decay: As the name suggests, time decay is based on recency. The older the post, the less value it has on Facebook, whereas new posts are rewarded with greater weighting. For example a photo posted an hour ago has decayed more than the one posted 5 minutes ago. Of course if the older photo has received a lot of likes, shares and comments it might still show on people's feeds, but the Time Decay Edgerank component won't be so large.

The biggest mistake many business pages make when it comes to time decay, is posting at times when their audience is not most active. It might be that your audience is mainly online during the evenings but you are at work (and posting) during the day. By the time your potential customers log on after dinner, your posts have already been replaced in their news feed with the latest pictures of cats, street brawl videos and incorrectly attributed quotes.

With a bit of experimentation, you can find the times of day that your posts get most interaction. If it's really inconvenient to post at this time, Facebook allows you to time your posts to go out at some point in the future, up to 6 months ahead.

Boosting Your Edgerank for Maximum Facebook Exposure

So that's Edgerank explained. Let's look at some final summary tips for taking advantage of it to boost your visibility:

Posting Quality Content: Posting quality content is central to your Facebook campaign, not least because of the associated Edgerank. In the back of your mind each time you are creating Facebook content should be the question "how engaging is this?". Will your audience truly find it useful, interesting and possibly share-worthy?

Format of your post: Keep in mind the Edge weight of your posts. Although status updates and images in particular tend to get people's attention users most, that doesn't mean a link to a good story won't work. But if you're going to post a link, write something to entice people to click on it to boost engagement. Try experimenting with different post formats, topics, adding a call to action, questions and anything else your audience will be interested in to see how each affects the success of your posts. You'll start to notice that your posts which don't drive high interactions usually don't deserve to - most are likely too inwardly focussed and fail to be of any interest to the audience.

Get noticed with frequent posts: There is no single 'correct' frequency for Facebook posting, because the most suitable frequency depends so heavily on your market and post topic. People might be happy to hear from a pizza restaurant or photographer every day or more, whereas we probably don't need (or want) to hear from an accountant every day, for example. You want to post frequently enough to be in the people's minds without boring them enough for them to click Hide Story (bad for Edgerank) or, worse, unliking you altogether.

Statistics show that more than 90% fans never come back to visit a Facebook page once they've liked it, so making sure that your posts get to your fans' feeds is crucial for maintaining your relationship. Using common sense to decide the frequency of your posts is a great place to start.

Follow rules: While a little bit of controversy and 'spice' is generally good for engagement and keeping interest in your page high, it's important not to overdo it or alienate any segment of your audience - unless that's part of your positioning, of course!

Interaction with fans: Social media should be a two-way street and it's important to try to create open conversations with your fans. This can be tough to begin with as you experiment and find the sort of topics that get your audience talking, but this experience can help you identify misunderstandings or discover topics that your fans are really passionate about that you can use in your wider marketing. And remember: when you respond to a fan, not only do you invest your time and effort in an actual brand-customer relation but you are also investing in the affinity of that fan's *friends*.

Stay updated, be involved and experiment: Any serious social media marketing student will begin to see Facebook on two levels: on one level you have your personal use, friends, cats and so on (you are the consumer), but on a deeper level you'll begin to notice how it works and start to see beneath the surface. Study your competitors and which posts drive most interaction. Follow big brands like Starbucks to see what they're up to, and follow technology blogs like Tech Crunch and Mashable to see what those who really understand Edgerank are doing. It's also worth following a number of the 'viral' pages - those that show up in your news feed despite the fact you have no relationship with them other than one of your friends interacted with their post. These pages are run by some of the smartest marketers with a game plan to monetise the page or build huge Edgerank.

Facebook Advertising

As a social media marketer it is absolutely vital that you have an understanding of Facebook advertising. The opportunity Facebook advertising gives us to target people with particular interests is absolutely unparalleled in its ease and low cost to anything else in the history of advertising. Yes, it's really THAT good.

Tim built an entire information marketing business thanks mainly to less than $1,000 of highly targeted Facebook advertising. Don't listen to General Motors and the other big brands publicly complaining that Facebook ads are ineffective and expensive - they are confusing their own ignorance of basic online marketing with Facebook being an ineffective advertising platform. The cost can be extremely low if you get the message right and understand how to build affinity with your audience.

But all the different features and options can seem a little overwhelming for new marketers, which is why Facebook itself offers great guidance on how to start a successful ad campaign. We're not going to patronise you by explaining the steps to setting up these different types of advert in brain-dead detail, as Facebook has excellent guidelines and an intuitive advertising process, but where we can offer tips and shortcuts we'll mention them.

There are Facebook's 5 types of On-page advertising:

Facebook Ad: These are the classic ads that appear on the right of your profile and Newsfeed. These are 'display' type adverts that don't usually have any social interaction component by default, but rather comprise of a picture and small amount of text enticing you to click. These ads give you the option to send the user to an external page (for example your website) or your own Facebook business page.

The key to these ads is an eye catching picture. Without this, your audience won't even see the text and you'll have no opportunity to appeal for the user's click. We feel our eyes drawn to certain types of picture, and you'll notice that you're particularly drawn to faces and pictures with a sharp contrast. If you're interested in the power of a picture to improve click through rates on an advert and want to see the picture which generated us the most clicks per x impressions we've <u>ever</u> seen, Google "grey shirt girl". We once ran an experimental ad campaign on Linkedin using grey shirt girl as the photo. The ad generated so many clicks we had to turn it off as it quickly stopped being cost-effective. And for those who assume a gender bias once they see grey shirt girl, she proves equally as effective attracting clicks from male *and* female internet users. When you're testing

Facebook display ads, the photo should be the first thing you trial.

Sponsored Story: A sponsored story is simply a post that is generated because someone interacted with whatever you are promoting. So if you are promoting your business page and someone 'likes' it, this little piece of information will appear to that user's friends' Newsfeeds more frequently and more prominently than if it wasn't sponsored. The great thing about sponsored stories is that they appear in the feeds of people who may never have encountered your brand, but are now introduced to you through powerful social proof.

Promoted Posts: Got a specific offer, event announcement or image on your Facebook business page that you'd like to tell more people about? A promoted post is a great way to increase the visibility of that post. By promoting a post in this way, you essentially bypass Edgerank limitations and generate your desired level of visibility. Facebook gives you the option to select the recently posted content you want to promote, and the number of impressions (views) that you want to buy. Just make sure that the post is suitably *valuable* to your audience - some of the promoted posts from big brands (about such fascinating subjects as their TV adverts, new price plans etc) are so far from being interesting we can't help but call some of them out publicly by commenting on the ads suggesting they read a certain book on social media.

Sponsored App: If your business has it's own application on Facebook, you can promote this app through the promoted app option. The idea behind this is to make stories about users engaging with your app more prominent in their friends' Newsfeeds, using social proof to drive curiosity and, as a result, more app users. We won't go into too much detail about this here as it's not likely to be relevant to most small and medium-sized business owners.

Event Sponsorship: If your business uses events to collect leads or drive new business, you can use Facebook advertising to increase visibility in the run up to the event. Particularly useful are the geographic targeting options that allow you to limit the catchment area of your ads to a particular town, city or radius, preventing wasted ad spend and making sure you're attracting only those with a reasonably high chance of being able to attend.

Targeting and Optimization of Facebook Ads

Now that we've seen what types of advertising Facebook offers it's time to explore the target and optimisation options at our disposal for making sure our ad campaigns are as effective and profitable as possible.

Facebook has made our lives easy by giving us the option of targeting our audience from country to city, as well as by age, gender, marital status, education level or even specific educational establishment (useful if you are using your past university to build affinity). So if you know your business really appeals to a specific demographic, you don't need to waste money advertising to people who aren't in that group.

By far the most awesome thing that Facebook has done for marketers is to let us find our target audience based on their interests. We can select as many interests as we want and target the people on Facebook who have the same interests or have liked pages related to those interests.

In the past this level of targeting was restricted to expensive media with long lead times like print magazines, where an advert could cost thousands, or trade shows where only a small proportion of each target audience would be present. To have this level of targeting available at such a low price online is very exciting, and with such low cost we've seen some very exciting ROI on well-optimised Facebook ad campaigns.

The speed with which Facebook ads can be tested is also good news for savvy marketers because it means we can tune our campaign for maximum profit much faster than if we needed to wait 2-3 months between each advert iteration. As we move into the era of graph search and Facebook continues to collect more and more data about its users, we'll see the targeting capabilities developed even further.

As an aside, much of the privacy issues Facebook has are nothing to do with some evil desire to snoop on its users' private lives, but instead give advertisers more information to help them target ads better. It's rare to find Facebook advertisers who have any problem whatsoever with Facebook collecting personal data, because it can be so profitable to those who use it in well-planned ad campaigns.

Fine Tuning Your Targeting

In order to make sure that your audience is large enough for your lead generation goals, Facebook will give you an approximate total audience size as you refine your targeting options.

Depending on the type of campaign you are running, you might want to fine tune the people that see your advert. Facebook allows you to choose any of the following five:

Anyone: This option will show your ad to everyone that falls under within your target audience based on their likes and interests, *even if they have no prior connection to your business*. This is useful for adverts where the social proof element of seeing that a friend liked or interacted with your page isn't important enough to justify limiting your ad's reach. For example, let's say that you were running an ad campaign offering a free brochure for a wedding venue to women who were engaged, you probably would choose the 'anyone' category so as not to limit the number of brides-to-be who saw your ad.

People connected to your brand: This will allow you to target people who already like your page. A good use for this can be promoting special offers, new services or for promoting content that you hope they will want to share with *their* friends.

People not connected to your brand: This can be useful if you are running a campaign to drive likes or incentivise *new* customers to do business with you through a welcome offer or promotional coupon.

Advanced Targeting: If you know your audience well and want to target fans of particular pages who you've identified as highly relevant potential customers, using advanced targeting to do this can make good sense. You also have the option to negatively target fans of particular pages - for example selling Manchester United merchandise to people who 'like' local rivals Manchester City could result in a lot of wasted advertising spend...

Friends of connections: Use this to target people whose friends are already fans of your business page. This allows you to use social proof to boost the relevance of your ad. Clearly if people see that a friend has already liked your page, this will usually increase their perception of the page (depending on the friend!).

Payment Options

When it comes to paying for your ads, Facebook gives you a few different options. It can auto-optimize your campaign budget for clicks or impressions, which means that Facebook will automatically set your cost-per-click (CPC) or cost per thousand impressions (CPM) to spend your budget the 'best' way possible while getting you the most number of clicks or impressions. Facebook also lets you choose to set your CPC or CPM manually. We usually prefer the control of choosing manually, but if you are not the sort to test and experiment with different bids, then having this done automatically is a convenient option.

Twitter

Using Twitter to market your business is a very different experience to using Facebook. Not only do you face restrictions on the type of posts (140 character text posts), but it has a very different feel and requires a different sort of approach.

5 Deadly mistakes to avoid on Twitter

Twitter is full of booboos and bad examples, and the examples of big brands 'getting it wrong' could fill an entire book. Everyone slows down for a car crash though, so let's take a look at some good examples of how NOT to do Twitter so you can avoid making the same mistakes:

1. Make sure you're signed in to the right account when tweeting! Accidentally tweeting something from your company twitter account when you meant to tweet it from your personal account can be a recipe for disaster. We saw what KitchenAid did back when President Obama's grandma passed away. One of the employees accidentally tweeted "Obama's gma even knew it was going 2 be bad! She died 3 days b4 he became president. #nbcpolitics"

Obviously it's bad enough to tweet insensitive things about family death, but then doing that from your company account? That's social media suicide. The horrendous text-lingo surely didn't help either...

2. Having no strategy for communicating with your audience. When @amberkarnes accused Urban Outfitters of stealing designs for their clothing, the 'Twitterverse' jumped on the story. Urban Outfitters clearly had no strategy to respond in this type of situation, issuing a half baked attempt to clear up the mess. It was nowhere near enough though and the brand lost 17,000 followers. Both #urbanoutfitters and #thieves were trending in just a few hours.

3. Rely too heavily on automation or 'bots'. Many companies and individuals use annoying auto-messaging software to message new followers, but sometimes the automation becomes much more public. Bank of America experienced the wrath of angry Twitter users recently when it misguidedly tried to diffuse the complaints of an angry dad who'd had his house foreclosed. When other Tweeters joined in calling out the bank displaying their anger at the repossessions going on, the bank started sending out generic messages: "We'd be happy to review your account with you to address any concerns. Please let us know it you need assistance. ^sa". This didn't really help the situation which quickly got out of hand. The bank later explained that actually the tweets came from live responders, but by then the damage was done.

4. Trying to make money by taking advantage of sad events. @tweetbox360 tweeted "Remember Amy Winehouse by downloading the ground-breaking 'Back

to Back' over at Zune" It's a fine line between taking advantage of opportunities to sell more and being insensitive and the twittersphere doesn't take kindly to the former.

5. Tweeting about political or religious matter. Just don't go there...

Attracting More Followers On Twitter

There are two ways to get lots of Twitter followers: the real way or the fake way.

Websites like Fiverr offer a huge number of follower boosting packages for very low cost. This can seem like a fantastic shortcut to get lots of new fans to market to. However, usually these followers are either automated bots or fake accounts and offer absolutely no benefit to your business at all (other than an inflated follower count).

If you would prefer to grow your following legitimately, here are our top tips for attracting new followers:

Tweet Regularly: Just as with Facebook, the frequency of your posts can make a big difference to your success. On Twitter, due to the immediacy and much faster decay (it's very unlikely that a Twitter user will see one of your posts from more than a few hours ago), your audience will generally put up with a much higher post frequency. Without Facebook's Affinity and Edge Weight factors, your tweets rely on recency to appear. If your audience spans the globe you'll need to bear in mind the times of day each country is most likely to be using Twitter so you can time your tweets accordingly. It's also acceptable to repost the same tweet during the day in order to boost its visibility, although clearly this can be overdone as well!

Follow People: Many brands and individuals maintain a habit of following back people who follow them. You can use this to grow your follower base by following others in your industry hoping that when they see the notification of your follow, they'll decide to follow back. It's worth remembering that they'll see your tagline when deciding whether or not to follow you, so of course it's extremely important that your tagline reflects not only who you are and what you do, but indicates a benefit for those who will be following you: "follow for the latest developments in medical recruiting", for example.

It's important to be aware that profiles which embark on campaigns following hundreds of users in a short space of time and have a very high 'follow to follower' ratio can be blocked by Twitter, as they try to crack down on spam profile creation.

Interact: If people are retweeting you, mentioning you or generally just reaching out to you, it's good social media etiquette to respond. It is good manners to thank people for following and retweeting you on Twitter, and you can start messages with the follower's @handle in order to stop the tweet showing up on the rest of your audience's feeds (unless they already follow your new follower).

Influencer Outreach: As mentioned previously, industry influencers can be a great source of exposure for your business Twitter account. Reaching out, sharing your content with them, retweeting them, mentioning them can all put you on their radar and increase the chance of getting a response or reciprocal follow.

Use Relevant Hashtags: Using hashtags that are relevant to your industry or that your audience is already using (for example conference hashtags) can put your tweets in front of a large and targeted audience. If your tweets add value and demonstrate your expertise, this type of exercise can pick you up a lot of new relevant followers which over time you can begin to build relationships with.

Just like Facebook, Twitter marketing doesn't have to stop at organic promotion. It too has a paid advertising platform which is worth experimenting with if you find an audience receptive to your tweets.

Twitter Advertising

Twitterizing 101

Twitter advertising (Twitterizing) comes with many features that not only suit large global brands, but also small and medium enterprises. Let's take a look at the process of setting up and targeting a Twitter ad campaign.

Step 1. Setting up Twitter advertising
To get access to Twitter advertising head to business.twitter.com. At the time of writing, Twitter has three different methods of advertising:

1. **Promoted account** that lets you promote your brand's Twitter account

2. **Promoted tweets** that lets you promote the tweets you want your followers to see.

3. **Promoted trends** that lets your trend be displayed in the top of the list on Twitter.com and Twitter's mobile apps.

Let's take a look at each of these in turn:

Promoted Accounts
The aims of promoted accounts are to raise visibility of your profile and attract more followers. It's worth bearing in mind that having more followers, while it seems like an excellent goal, doesn't necessarily mean *anything* for the profitability of your Twitter marketing, although it does go some way to boost your credibility.

Twitter promotes the accounts of advertisers choosing this option by giving them preferential placement in search results, in the 'who to follow' tab and in 'similar to user' tabs on the website and in the Twitter mobile apps. Clearly the effectiveness of this sort of advertising will depend greatly on the appeal of your profile and the perceived value of following you, so our advice is usually to establish your page first demonstrating that your posts are good quality and likely to be of interest to those who find you through the promoted profile ads.

Let's see how we can enable the Promote account feature:

- Choose 'Promoted Account' from the options after signing up for Twitter advertising at ads.twitter.com.
- You can now choose an existing Twitter account if you want to target people similar to that user's followers. For example, if one of your competitors is highly visible and has a large Twitter following that you would like to attract some of, you can enter their Twitter handle and target your ads at their followers.
- The next step is adding 'Interest Categories' that you'd like to target. To help you choose, click the Browse Categories button to see a list of the categories Twitter identifies. Usually we recommend starting small and targeting only topics you are fairly sure will drive high engagement. Once you see what sort of results you are getting from the very most relevant

audience, you can always decide to broaden your net out from there.

- Choose the location you want to target, which is crucial in avoiding wasted ad spend if you're a local business.
- You can also choose to target your ads by gender. Yes, compared to Facebook's in depth demographic selection choosing gender is not exactly game changing, but for many businesses it does allow them to trim down their target audience by 50%.
- Next up it's time to talk money. You'll need to set a daily budget which caps the ad cost so you don't get caught out. You can then optionally set a campaign budget, which would stop the campaign once it's reached.
- The Maximum Spend Per Follow is a sort of bidding system that determines the visibility of your ads. The more you are willing to spend each time someone follows you, the more visibility Twitter will give your promoted profile. In our experience, the amount you actually pay per follow tends to be quite a lot less, particularly if you are targeting your ads quite narrowly. This is just as well, because paying their 'suggested bid' of $2.50 - $3 is a very expensive way to grow your following!
- Once you've saved your campaign, you can choose to Launch it or modify.

- Viola! And that's that! Your Twitter profile will now be recommended to people with similar interests you've just chosen.

If you're used to Facebook's sophisticated ad targeting then the simplicity (some say *oversimplicity*) of Twitter's advert targeting might seem a little limiting. Facebook's user data is virtually unmatched (save for governments, intelligence agencies and, worst of all, Google) which gives Zuckerberg & co a much larger pool of information to target ads. Twitter, on the other hand, knows relatively little about it's users so the ad targeting options are much more limited.

Promoted Tweets

Promoted Tweets are exactly what they sound like, giving you the ability to increase the visibility of your tweets in search results and Twitter users' timelines.

Once you log into the Twitter ads dashboard at ads.twitter.com, click start a new campaign and choose 'promoted tweets' you'll see the following targeting options:

- Keywords. Targeting keywords allows you to identify your ad audience by the things they talk about, search for or engage with (retweet, @reply, follow etc)
- Interests and followers gives a broader and less focussed audience, based on people who follow certain accounts.

In most cases, we recommend ROI-driven businesses target keywords rather than interests and followers, which is a softer option most often suited to big brands seeking publicity or raising general awareness. For most small and medium-sized businesses (and in fact many larger brands) this sort of approach usually doesn't generate the sort of ROI that a well-focussed keyword-based campaign does.

If you choose the Keyword option, you'll see that there are now two choices for where your ads will appear:

- Search results, giving your tweet extra prominence when users search for your keywords. Here the type of searches you want to target (the keywords you choose) can make a big difference to the sort of results (followers, interactions, RTs etc) you get. As always with Twitter, our advice here is to start out by testing very narrowly-targeted phrases and broaden your net as you start to see results. The temptation is there to cast out a wide net (choosing lots of almost-relevant search terms) but often this can lead to very low conversion rates.
- Users' Timelines - a relatively new option, allowing you to advertise in the timelines of people who use your keywords in their tweets.

The next step is entering the keywords you'd like to target. Just like Facebook, Twitter helpfully suggests additional keywords once you start entering some of your own. The little blue dot next to the keyword illustrates typical global daily search volume, allowing you to compare the popularity of each keyword.

Once you start typing in the keywords, you'll notice that there are different targeting options for each phrase. 'Match in any order' means that the ad will be triggered by any combination of these words, whereas "phrase" matched means that the exact phrase has to be used before the ads will be triggered. The negative options allow you to avoid tweets or searches using a particular phrase. For example, a nationwide plumbing company wanting to offer free boiler repair quotes to people who mention the phrase "boiler breakdown" might want to negatively target the word "DIY" so as to avoid targeting those who have chosen to do it themselves. Likewise website designers who want visibility in the newsfeeds of people who tweet about websites might want to choose the negative phrase "free website" to avoid advertising to those who are unwilling to pay for a website.

Location targeting Promoted Tweets is the same as for Promoted Accounts, covered above.

One extra option available to Promoted Tweet advertisers is to narrow their audience according to device. Here you can choose from desktops or mobile devices based on operating system. App and smartphone game developers will find this particularly useful as it allows them to serve ads with links to the relevant app store only to users of the right devices.

The next step is to choose the tweets you want to promote. Once you've targeted your audience, creating this tweet is the piece of the Twitter advertising puzzle that deserves the most attention. You'll see that Twitter gives you the option to 'Automatically Promote' your tweets based on those that get high engagement, but this is a very lazy option for non-serious marketers. In the fabulous words of Brian Tracy, "this is not for you".

Your promoted tweet should be designed specifically to drive a response from the reader. Fuzzy goals like 'awareness' and 'visibility' should be left to businesses that have a fixed marketing budget each year to waste on low return advertising. Your ad should contain the following elements:

- A benefit statement, explicitly stating the benefit the reader will experience by using your service
- A call to action telling the reader what to do in order to claim this benefit.

Remember that your advert audience did not open Twitter to read about your business, and they're attention is being pulled in a thousand different directions. You need to grab them quickly and make them an offer they can't refuse. You can then build rapport and over time grow your relationship in order to make them a regular customer. This is the basis of lead generation advertising, the primary form of advertising used by businesses who need it to pay a return.

The ideal promoted tweet offers something of high perceived value in exchange for something of low perceived value (or free). 'Free' is a very useful tool when trying to attract people's attention and motivate a response, and can be the basis of a very profitable ad campaign. A free report, free audit, free muffin with a coffee, a free extra night when booking 2 nights, a free sample; provided that you have a well thought-out funnel to turn the advert respondents into customers, you'll be surprised just how much you can afford to give away.

Keep an eye out for our upcoming book 'Profitable Internet Marketing' for a really in depth look at lead generation online.

Promoted Trends

As mentioned before, trends are one of the features that are unique to Twitter. Twitter shows users in each location what the 10 most popular words or hashtags being tweeted about at that moment. Buy paying for a promoted trend, brands can buy onto this list and thus get a hashtag of their choice in front of people watching the trends list. For example: #Crazy4Good (Coca Cola's campaign).

Currently promoted trends are exclusive to companies with an account managed by a Twitter ad rep, and are not available to the general public.

Blogging

A business blog is a really useful tool in a profitable social media marketing campaign as it gives you a central focus point for all your social sharing. It's a great platform to publish your ideas, create networking opportunities and also boost your SEO and search ranking, all on your own terms. In addition, it shows visitors to your website that your business is alive and kicking, as well as showing them what you stand for and why you're different.

Think of your blog as the central hub online which all your social media activity feeds into.

It's often said that the hardest part of blogging is starting, and there are usually three main barriers that prevent most blogs from moving beyond the idea stage:

The first barrier is waiting for the 'perfect' time to start. It's all too easy to imagine an ideal blog launch date at some point in the future, perhaps coinciding with a new product or service launch, the new year, or any other number of events. But bear in mind that your blog audience will take time to grow and you'll take time to find your stride with posting. When it comes to starting, there really is no time like the present. So if a blog is part of your social media strategy (which it should be in most cases), commit to starting immediately and then force yourself to do it.

The second barrier to getting started with blogging is the worry that your writing will be judged by your peers, customers and the wider world. The truth? Generally people are too caught up in their own lives to spend much time thinking about you, and when reading your blog they'll be far less judgemental than you think. Any judgements they *do* form will be more a reflection of their own attitudes than your writing, so you really can't let this get in your way.

Finally, many business owners worry that they won't have enough to talk about for their blog to be interesting. What they fail to recognise is that for people *outside* your company or industry, a lot of your insights you take for granted might be completely new and very interesting. If you have information that can move your audience closer to their goals in any way, what might seem mundane or obvious to *you*, to *them* could be the most useful thing they read that week.

So what's the key to overcoming these three barriers? Once you accept that your blog will never be 'perfect' and that you'll continue to improve and develop your own style as you go, the pressure is off. Just do it.

Getting Started with Blogging

Your business blog will form the foundation of your social media presence, therefore it is really important to create the right framework to get you started on the right track. The blog framework you choose can have implications for everything, from what sort of audience you attract to how easy it is to maintain your blog on the go.

Let's go through the main considerations to help you get your blog off to the best start possible.

Blog Consideration Number 1 - The focus of your blog:

While the focus of your blog might seem straightforward to you, we're big fans of stating it explicitly and exploring if there are additional topics close to your audience's heart which you have expertise in. Other blogs in your industry can give you clues as to the sort of posts that your market finds most interesting and relevant, as can the topics that appear regularly in industry publications such as magazines, newsletters and conferences.

If you're a business owner you might find that some of your staff have an expertise or interest in a certain area that you lack, and inviting them to demonstrate this knowledge on the company blog can have the additional benefit of giving your employees the pride of being recognised for their expertise.

So when planning your blog's focus, be wary of defining this too narrowly.

Blog Consideration Number 2 - Pick a platform:

If you already have a website with a built-in blog functionality (for example if you use Wordpress), then your decision about the platform to use is easy. For everybody else, the options for creating an 'add on' blog can seem overwhelming. You have basically two choices: hosted and self-hosted. The difference is quite simple: Sself-hosted blogs live on your own hosting, whereas hosted blogs live on someone else's hosting. Because you'll have a higher level of access to your own hosting than you would to someone else's, self hosted blogs generally give you more control over things like the domain name (www.domainname.com), the blog layout, and the look and feel. The downside is that having a self-hosted blog requires more setup and you are responsible for the ongoing maintenance. Of all the self-hosted blog platforms available, Wordpress is by far the most popular for reasons we'll explore later on.

Hosted blogs on the other hand (e.g. Tumblr or Google's Blogger) tend to be much more simple to set up for those without technical experience, and you can get started within a matter of minutes. The downside of hosted blogs is that you sacrifice many of the customisation features of a self-hosted blog in return for the convenience of having it hosted for you. Wordpress also offers a hosted blog platform with simple setup that *does* give you some of these customisation features, but they come at a price significantly higher than if you're hosting your Wordpress site yourself, and there are still features you won't have access to.

We almost always recommend self-hosted Wordpress blogs for businesses and there are a number of reasons. The design control that self-hosted Wordpress gives you and the number of pre-made themes available, means that you get a great looking blog with very little effort. The Wordpress platform is very easy to use, and we find that even our most technically challenged clients are comfortable with creating new posts, adding pictures and trying out new themes once they've spent a bit of time getting familiar with it. Using a self-hosted Wordpress blog also means you can use your own domain name and integrate it with your main website, giving a much more professional appearance than sending visitors off to a third-party website.

There are also a number of SEO benefits to using Wordpress which are beyond the scope of this book, but if you're interested check out our other book 'How to Get to the Top of Google' for a more in depth look at SEO and Wordpress. If you need some help setting up a Wordpress blog please contact us at Exposure Ninja and we'll be happy to get you up and running.

Blog Consideration Number 3 - Branding:

Clearly your blog branding needs to match or at least reflect the branding of your company's website in order to give a feeling of coherence. Most blog platforms will give you space to put a logo and choose the colours used, and any customisation beyond that is down to the particular platform and theme that you're using.

Remember that in social media, perception is everything and it's important that your blog looks the part if you want to build credibility. Having a professional designer create the graphics and layout for your blog can be a wise investment if it saves you hours battling the settings yourself trying to get things looking *almost* professional. Just as with your main website, it's important to be completely honest with yourself about whether your blog really looks professional enough. If you want to be perceived as a reputable quality company, your blog and website has to reflect this immediately.

The Exposure Ninja designers and developers can work with you on every aspect of your blog's appearance so if you get stuck we are here to help.

Blog Consideration Number 4 - The Content:

Now that your blog has a great design and is ready to roll, it's time to think about the most important part - the content!

We talked about understanding your audience earlier in this book, and clearly this is the first step for any targeted marketing effort, including blogging. A social media-friendly blog attracts comments, shares and referral traffic so it's a good idea to cover the sort of topics that your potential customers are already thinking and talking about, as well as solving their problems or giving them new angles on issues relevant to them.

Blogs often use categories to sort their content and you can plan these categories in advance, using them to guide your content creation and make sure that the topics you cover with your posts are all useful to your audience.

Remember that you don't necessarily have to create all the content on your blog yourself. If someone in your team has more time or experience with content creation, outsourcing the writing to them can be an efficient and effective move.

The ongoing content creation is where most blogs begin to slide. What starts with an earnest attempt at regular posting becomes semi-regular to infrequent, until your blog readers start to spot tumbleweed. The dates of the 'Latest Posts' give the game away and bear testament to a once-eager blogger who gave up before they reached the finish line. Creating (and sticking to) a schedule is a great way to force yourself to come up with new blog posts. Whether you want to blog daily, weekly or monthly, committing yourself to sitting down and coming up with a new blog post will be the key to keeping your blog alive. If it gets left until you have some spare time, it won't get done!

Using visual content

Including pictures and videos in your blog posts can help attract clicks when the posts are shared on social media, as well as boosting engagement with the posts themselves. Posts with pictures get more space when shared on Facebook, as well as peaking your audience's interest when they see the post on your site. Where possible avoid using pictures that are clearly stock images because this screams 'generic'. Opt instead for original photography, artwork or infographics where possible.

Just how much time and energy you have to put into sourcing the images for your blog depends heavily on your business and market. A local plumber will find that iPhone pictures of recent plumbing jobs give him or her a lot more credibility amongst their audience, whereas a large multinational training company would be expected to use professionally taken photos of for example.

Some businesses will struggle to identify what sort of visual content they can use in their blog posts. But whatever your product or service, there is *something* you can show your audience that illustrates to them the benefit of what you're offering, represents an end result or reminds them of a pain that they're experiencing.

Blogging SEO

Keywords

Search engines can be a fantastic (and free) source of traffic to your blog, and ultimately leads and customers for your business. In order to maximise your blog's visibility in search results, it helps to have a basic understanding of SEO (search engine optimisation) and how to use keywords.

Keywords are the words and phrases your audience uses to search for your product, service or benefit. For example, a women's shoe shop might sell a range of sandals for weddings. After talking to their customers and doing some research online, the owner identifies that the phrase "white wedding sandals" is really popular and matches with their most popular shoes in this category. They might decide to target the phrase "white wedding sandals" by writing a blog post called "The Perfect White Wedding Sandals". This post could talk about recent trends in wedding footwear, the different white wedding sandals the shop sells, the benefits of each type and considerations when choosing a pair. The words "white", "wedding" and "sandals", the phrase "white wedding sandals" and related phrases such as "white wedding shoes" would appear throughout the article giving Google and the other search engines a really clear idea that the subject of this blog post was… you've guessed it… white wedding sandals.

Here are some quick keyword tips for your blog posts:

- **Use just one or two keywords in each blog post:** By focussing on a narrowly targeted set of keywords ("White wedding sandals" vs "wedding shoes", which is a lot less specific), you make it more likely that your posts will rank highly in search engines. It's also worth considering *commercial intent*: people searching for white wedding sandals are likely to be more ready to buy than those searching for wedding shoes, who are probably still in the research phase because they haven't yet identified the type of shoes they're looking for.
- **Use your keywords in the post title:** Titles have a huge importance in SEO, so including your keywords in your title (and early on, if possible) will really help boost your ranking as well as show your audience clearly what your post is about.
- **Use the keywords in the blog post:** Obviously it's important to use the keywords in your blog post, but it's also a good idea to include variations and related phrases as these give the search engines a broader understanding of the subject of your post.
- **Be aware of keyword density and post length:** One of the most common mistakes made by those new to SEO is overusing their keywords under the assumption that more = better. It's important to keep in mind that the main audience for your site is the readers, not the search engines, and nothing should be done

to the blog which jeopardises your readers' experience. 'Keyword Stuffing', as the overuse of keywords is commonly known, not only makes text difficult to read but is also looked down upon by Google. In order to be seen as high quality content, your posts should be a minimum of 300 words.

- **Image alt tags:** Don't forget to use keywords in your featured image's alt tags. Image alt tags are used to tell search engines what a picture is about, but also come in handy for SEO.

Meta Data

Many blog systems allow users to add a Meta description to their blog posts. This Meta description is often shown on social media and in search results to give people a clear idea of what your post is about. It's important to mention your keywords in this Meta description, and try to entice people to click and read more; treat the Meta description as an advert for your blog post.

The Power of a Good Headline

Irresistible headlines can be your greatest asset for getting your blog posts read, because most of your audience will decide whether or not to click on your post based on the headline alone. Clearly stating benefits, including keywords and speaking to your audience's core needs and desires are all powerful ways to boost the number of clicks your posts get.

If you're struggling to come up with an enticing headline, try brainstorming 10 or more on a sheet of paper, putting them aside overnight and revisiting in the morning.

Some examples of good headlines that use a mixture of curiosity and, yes, a little sensationalism to brighten up some potentially boring subjects :

- 6 Unbelievable Personal Injury Claims
- Britain: Bankrupt by 2014?
- College degrees with the highest starting salaries
- Eight surprising ways to increase productivity in the workplace
- Empty Pigs: Why banks have given up on savers
- Starbucks asks customers to leave their guns at home

Growing Your Blog Audience

Over time, the goal for your blog is to attract new readers, build familiarity with them and eventually turn some into customers.

We'll now take a look at some ways to promote the content on your blog to make it more visible.

Encouraging Social Media Sharing: A social media strategy that relies in any way on your audience taking initiative or going out of their way to help you is doomed to failure. Make it easy for your readers to share your blog posts on social media with one click by including social sharing buttons right in the blog posts themselves. If you want to collect the email addresses of your readers, you can offer a subscription option that allows people to automatically receive your new blog posts. Again, make this as simple as possible. The more you force people to work for it, the fewer will bother.

Marketing Your Blog Posts on Your Own Social Channels: Once you've created your keyword-optimised blog post, included pictures, written a great headline and made it easy for people to share, it's time to get promoting it on your own channels. Linking to your new post from your company Facebook, Twitter, Google+ and Linkedin accounts can all bring you valuable traffic. If your content is very visual, posting pictures from your blog post on Pinterest can be another great source of visitors as the pictures will automatically link back to your blog.

Don't be afraid to outreach to industry figures, customers and peers asking for feedback on your post as well. If they like what they read and decide to share it, this can generate valuable referral traffic which you can then convert to regular visitors.

In addition to your own profiles on other social networks, there are some other neat strategies for promoting your content:

1. **Publish your blog on Kindle and get paid!** Head to https://kindlepublishing.amazon.com and sign up to publish your blog on Amazon's Kindle platform. While this won't be a huge source of revenue for anyone but the most high profile bloggers, it *can* be a great way to find new readers.

2. **Paid Content Syndication:** Outbrain.com, DemandStudios.com and other content syndication platforms allow you to pay to promote your blog posts on well-known sites. Paid advertising can be a fast way to attract new blog readers but before putting too much cash into advertising we recommend building up a following organically in order to prove that your posts are share-worthy, interesting and relevant enough to your audience that they will subscribe. Trying to paper over cracks with high advertising spend can be a costly route to failure so best to make sure your blog is working well for you first.

3. **Guest Posting:** Guest posting involves writing blog posts for other sites in order to get in front of their audience. Each post should be unique and targeted at the blog's native audience and reflect the sort of interests they have. If in doubt, ask the blog owner to suggest a topic that they

think their audience would be interested in reading about. Good guests posts aren't overly pitchy or promotional, but you'll want to include a link back to your blog in the article body as well as the bio/signature area.

4. **Advertising on Social Media:** If your blog posts are really high value, you might want to test using Facebook, Twitter or Linkedin advertising to get some traffic. As always with paid ads, test small and monitor the numbers really closely.

Google Plus

In June 2011, Google unveiled its social media platform, Google Plus. Many of us were somewhat sceptical about the need for yet another social media platform, but for Google the advertising opportunity that social media presents is just too important to ignore. It had to do *something*, and Google+ is the result.

Google of course did have one advantage over other startup social networks, in that it already had millions of users signed up for other Google services like Gmail, Adwords & Adsense, YouTube, Blogger and so on. These users could all have accounts set up very quickly, giving Google+ some impressive user numbers right out of the gate.

Whilst there are still elements of Google+ that are too confusing for anyone but experienced online marketing professionals to understand, adoption is growing as people begin to experiment. At Exposure Ninja we tend to set up Google+ for our clients' mostly for the SEO benefits, which are quite significant. Only time will tell how Google further integrates Google+ into search results, but the trend we're seeing through Search Plus Your World (SPYW), personalised results on Google maps and so on is that businesses with very active Google+ profiles and lots of connections are increasingly likely to be visible to other Google users. Adding products such as Google hangouts, automatically creating new Google+ accounts with registrations for other Google services and tying employee bonuses to Google+'s success are all signs that Google is very committed to its social network.

So without further delay, let's explore what Google Plus is and what features it has to offer that can benefit your business.

Marketing on Google Plus

As we'll see, Google+ offers us so many marketing tools it can be pretty overwhelming at first. Here's a Marketing on Google+ summary before we dive deeper into each area:

- Each business can set up their own Google+ profile page with details about their business, pictures and videos, reviews from customers and their stream of posts.
- Just like on Facebook and Twitter, you can use hashtags to categorise your posts and help them be found by people interested in those topics.
- The integration with Google's search results means you can use any 'social currency' you've built on Google+ to increase visits to your website through authorship markup and Google+ Local. We'll be looking at this in more detail later on.
- The 'Circles' functionality in Google+ allows you to closely control your privacy settings for each of your posts and audiences, unlike other social networks. Whether it's family photos, personal thoughts or business news, Circles allows you to choose which of your contacts can see your

updates so you don't have to be as worried about those party pictures damaging your workplace reputation!

- Like groups on Facebook and LinkedIn, Google Plus has Communities. These Communities are essentially groups of people with a common interest who have decided to share content with each other. From animals to yachting, the number of Communities is vast and you can also start your own. By being savvy and building relationships with the Community members over time you can begin to build awareness of your business without turning people off being too 'pitchy'. Communities can also be a great way to get some free market research.
- One of the coolest Google Plus features is Hangouts, which are essentially video conferences. Use customer hangouts to answer queries about your product and service or launch your new products without having to pay for live streaming or having to hire a venue.
- Close integration with your website means that it can be relatively easy to build your Google+ following with a small amount of technical know-how.

As you can see, on the surface Google+ offers a lot of promise and has perhaps the most potential of any of the social networks to be a really useful marketing tool. The only drawback is usage, as for most markets it's still very much a distant follower to Facebook and Twitter in terms of the number of active regular users.

Nonetheless we expect to see its popularity continue to grow over time and it's important to embrace Google+ now so as to be ready should it become truly mainstream.

Setting up a Google Plus Profile

To use Google+ for business, you'll first need a personal Google+ page. The process is extremely straightforward and generally well-explained, so to get started head over to plus.google.com and sign up, if you haven't already.

We'll look later on at Authorship Markup which allows you to link your website and your personal Google+ profile, which can really boost your site's traffic. If you intend to link your personal Google+ profile with your website, your profile picture will show up in the search results next to your site so you'll obviously want to make sure your personal profile pictures reflects the values of your business. This doesn't necessarily mean it has to be staid and boring, however:

<u>Face Painter Southampton</u>. Moxie's Magical Faces Children's and ...
facepaintersouthampton.co.uk/ ▾

by Zoe Moxie
Face Painter in Southampton Moxie's Magical Faces. Children's face painting, adult face painting, parties and games from experienced entertainer Zoe Moxie.

If you'll be primarily using Google+ for your business, then you'll want to gear your personal profile around positioning yourself in your industry, giving some background and showing potential customers a bit about the sort of person you are *outside* of work as well.

As always you want to aim for the most complete profile possible, so give as much information as you are comfortable with. Without a profile picture your profile won't be shown in search results, so it's really important to include a clear, recognisable headshot.

Setting up your Google+ Business Page

Now that you've done creating your personal profile, you'll want to create a page for your business.

- To get started, open the menu on the left hand side in your Google+ dashboard and click Pages.
- Click the Create a page button and select the most suitable category for your page – local business, product, brand, company, institution, organization, arts, entertainment, or other.
- There are many similarities between creating a profile and a page, but the pages offer a few additional touches like a link to your verified website. Other differences include an expanded 'story' section based on the type of page you've created. This allows you to give more details about things like the company background, your mission, and information about when the business was founded.
- If you have a brick-and-mortar business and you've chosen the 'local' page category, you can add an address listing for your business. This is really important as it can get you fantastic visibility on Google's map listings.

- Another major difference between a profile and a page is the ability to receive reviews of your business from customers. These reviews will be shown publicly, and an average review score can appear directly in the search results.

Integrating Google Plus with your Website

Integrating Google Plus with your business's website is a very good idea for a number of reasons, not least SEO and social proof. It can be fairly simple, and you don't have to be a tech geek in order to get some basic integration up and running:

The +1 Button

+1s are Google's version of Facebook likes. They are essentially a 'vote' from a visitor so embedding a +1 button on your site allows visitors to simply vote up your content. The number of +1s you've attracted is visible to other visitors, boosting social proof. In addition, each +1 is shared on that visitor's Google+ wall for those in their circles to see, similar to a Facebook like. This can help you generate additional 'viral' traffic.

But where Google +1s *really* shine is in integration with Google search to increase your visibility. Let's say that a potential customer called Tony visits your website, likes what he sees and decides to click your +1 button. This activity shows up on Tony's Google+ page and increases your +1 tally by one. The really cool bit happens when one of *Tony's* Google+ contacts (friends, coworkers, family) searches Google for a phrase relevant to your business. Your site will now receive preferential placement in the search results coupled with a notification that Tony has +1'd it.

So as you can see, the more +1s you have, the wider the network of Google users who are likely to see your site a) ranking higher on Google and b) recommended by someone they already know.

- Adding a +1 button on your website is fairly simple. Just visit https://developers.google.com/+/web/+1button/, customise the settings and copy the HTML snippet it creates for you.
- Now place that HTML on your website page where you want a +1 button to show.
- For the more technically advanced readers there are some additional options, but the basic functionality is sufficient for most.

Google Plus Badge

Google Plus badges are similar to +1 buttons, in that they give your visitors a chance to follow your Google+ page without leaving your website. They give more information about your profile or business page, display your profile and cover pictures and can show your tagline. Just like +1 buttons they're simple to generate and install:

- Visit https://developers.google.com/+/web/badge and customize the badge as you would like it to be displayed.

- Enter your Google Plus page URL in 'Google Plus user' box (or choose from the drop down box) and choose from the other settings on the page.
- Once you've set those options, you'll see an HTML code snippet right below the preview area of the badge. Copy it and put it wherever you want your badge to be shown on your website.
- Viola! You now have a cool Google Plus badge.

Other Website Integration Options

As you'll see from the Google+ Developers area (https://developers.google.com/+/) there are a wide variety of different Google+ widgets you can use on your website to increase the visibility of your Google+ profile, and new widgets are being added all the time. Which of these best help you grow your Google+ following depends to a great extent on your audience, website layout and the sort of content that you share. If in doubt, start with the humble +1 button and work from there.

Communities

As mentioned previously, Google+ Communities are not unlike forums or message boards in that they're a collection of people with a common interest who have agreed to receive updates from the other Community members. Being relatively new, most people have never heard about Google+ Communities, so you'll want to do some investigation into how widely your audience has adopted them before dedicating too much time into this strategy. Nevertheless I think it's important to be aware of the potential power of Communities so you can dip your toe in the water and see if they work for you.

Communities have the potential to be profitable to savvy social media marketers in a couple of ways:
1. They can be used to build and sell to an audience
2. They can be a great place to do targeted market research. You can use them to talk to customers and potential customers about what really matters to them

Just as with any audience building activity, the key focus when building or participating in a Google+ Community should always be on *providing value to the audience members*. This can be through informing them, making them feel significant, validating their beliefs or otherwise answering the question "what's in it for me to be a part of this Community?". This focus should not be forgotten. The Acme Industries owner that immediately heads to Google+, starts a Community called Acme Industries Ltd, spams it with adverts for the company's products and wonders why the Community never takes off is failing to comprehend a world outside his own head. Build value, respect and prominence first, harvest later.

If you're new to Communities it's a good idea to join some first before starting your own. Doing this allows you to observe what makes a Community particularly active or not and the sort of content that gets decent levels of interaction. You'll also be able to start building relationships with people. Once you've made a name for yourself in some existing and relevant Communities, bring your contacts over to your own Community.

So what sort of Communities should you be joining? Initially while you're finding your feet, it doesn't matter too much and you can afford to be liberal choosing any that your customers and potential customers might be spending time in. These might be Communities focused on solving a particular problem or need (School Holiday Activities, Weight Loss) or Communities for an interest, hobby or profession (Tea Lovers, Hair Stylists).

Private Communities require administrator approval before joining, but public Communities allow you walk right in and get sharing. Once you're familiar with the sort of content that seems to attract +1s inside these Communities, you can begin to post your own and measure the response.

LinkedIn

LinkedIn is the business-oriented social network of choice for most professionals. There are now over 225 million active users with two new users signing up every second. Long used by recruiters and headhunters, recent research has shown that some employers look at LinkedIn profiles *before* reading resumes, indicating just how deeply it has penetrated the world of business. With 2.6 million companies already having their own LinkedIn page, it all presents a pretty compelling argument for getting involved.

But what sort of opportunities are available to small and medium sized businesses on the network, and what sort of companies stand to benefit the most?

On the whole, most of the businesses that use LinkedIn marketing are B2B because of LinkedIn's audience and the mindframe they're in while they're on the site. That doesn't mean that it *can't* be profitable for B2C companies, but work-related products and services do tend to find greater success.

Similarly to Facebook, LinkedIn marketing for businesses is done via a business profile page. Through this page you can post status updates and links to content elsewhere on the web, as well as job openings. It's safe to say that the company profile has taken some cues from Facebook business pages, and the same interaction options (like, share & comment) are available to your audience. If you're new to LinkedIn marketing but have experience with Facebook, it will all feel very familiar…

Your Company's Voice

Because people tend to be in a business frame of mind when using LinkedIn, on the whole the sorts of posts from companies on the network tend to be more professional, conservative and, well, business-like. Engagement levels also tend to be (on the whole) lower, so don't judge your page a failure if you don't get the sort of sharing, liking and commenting activity that you're used to receiving on Facebook.

Although your audience on LinkedIn might appear different to your audience on any of the other social networks, it's important to remember that they are still human and thus are driven by the same principles as anywhere else. Headlines still need to arouse curiousity, short text descriptions still need to emphasise the benefits of doing business with you, and you should still allow some of the personality behind the business to come through in your communication. And remember: just because it's for professionals doesn't mean it should be boring.

Using LinkedIn Groups

LinkedIn groups can be a fantastic way of collecting leads, peers, customers or just about anyone else on

LinkedIn. Similar in principle to Google+ Communities covered elsewhere in this book, LinkedIn groups warrant some serious study for businesses who have a significant potential audience on the site.

There are already thousands of specialist groups for every industry, sector or problem imaginable (and plenty that are unimaginable), but starting your own group can give you perceived authority and clout which you can use to your adantage later on.

In order to promote a webinar we conducted with a client running an information product business in the recruitment industry, the company boss took to LinkedIn groups and started to make a name for himself in order to build an audience. From calling out established industry figures, to prophesising about future trends as well as generally stirring up controversy Once the group members were familiar with him, he set up his own group and began to bring members over. This boosted his credibility and the experience from interacting in the established groups helped him to identify a successful angle likely to catch the attention of his audience whilst also keeping him 'on side;. Once his own group had a decent membership, he could use the group to promote his own online events, books and courses.

Many groups on LinkedIn are set to Private, requiring membership approval by the group manager. Generally these groups tend to be higher quality because the

manager is filtering out the irrelevant members and the group retains a high level of integrity.

To begin with, just as with Google+ Communities, we recommend that you join a range of LinkedIn groups relevant to your audience. Spending some time observing and noticing which types of post tend to drive high interaction is really useful research for your own group and help you hit the ground running. It also gives you a chance to build relationships with some of the most prominent figures in the LinkedIn groups, whose authority you can then piggyback.

If you're new to LinkedIn and would like to find some suitable groups to join, you can start by typing in relevant keywords in the search bar and choosing Groups from the drop down menu. The search results will show you the largest and most active groups that those in your network are a part of, and you can follow this paper trail to find groups with a suitable level of activity in topics relevant to you.

Starting Your Own LinkedIn Group

When the time comes for you to start your own group, choose Groups from the Interests menu at the top of the page, and click the button to Create a new group. On the set up page you'll see options for naming your group, writing the description, giving a URL as well as setting the picture and choosing whether the group is closed (new members require approval and discussions aren't publicly visible) or open (new members can join instantly and all discussions are public.

If your main goal is to raise visibility of yourself, your product or your brand, then usually creating an open group is the best option because new customers won't need to wait for your approval before they can start seeing the effects of your influence.

For the focus of your group, you'll need to balance having a wide net to attract enough members with focussing the group enough that the members are good potential customers for you and to avoid the group discussions becoming too off-topic. The name of your group is extremely important and the most popular groups tend to have very descriptive yet broad names. Be aware that the group name and logo will be the most visible components across LinkedIn, so users should be able to immediately understand what the group is about and how it is relevant to them from just the title alone. Avoid use of your company name unless it is a genuine attraction to potential customers.

Just as with the other social media marketing strategies in this book, seek to add value to the group/market/audience *first*. Once people are familiar with you, they'll be far more responsive to any marketing messages you push out. If you're the group facilitator, there's a perceived authority that is very powerful and gives you a high level of credibility, but that authority must be used wisely and sparingly.

The logo or picture you give your group is also very important and gives potential members an indication as to how high-value and well-established the group is. A homemade logo or photograph that is not clearly visible in thumbnail form will give the group an amateurish look from the word go, and for the very small cost of having someone design a group logo for you you can give a much better first impression.

LinkedIn Advertising

LinkedIn's advertising platform, like it's profiles, is quite similar to Facebook. The data it has on its users is similar in scope (although clearly more work-oriented) so the targeting options available are much richer. A lot of the advertising done on LinkedIn is recruitment, but that doesn't stop other businesses from targeting the LinkedIn audience whether selling consultancy, marketing help or even franchises.

It's not just businesses who are already successful with LinkedIn who are able to attract leads and customers from the ad platform either. Experimentation and testing is the only reliable way to find out if, and how well, LinkedIn ads can work for your business.

Let's go through the process of setting up a LinkedIn advertising campaign for the first time:

- To sign up for advertising, go to linkedin.com/ads and click on 'Start Now' button.

You'll see the option to create an ad or promote an update. For this example we'll be creating an ad.

- Before setting up your campaign, decide whether you're advertising a business or yourself. If you're advertising on behalf of your business, you'll want to set up a Business Advertising account by clicking the drop down menu in the top right hand corner. If your company is already on LinkedIn, you can link it at this stage as well as choose your currency.
- You'll need to choose a name for your ad campaign, select the destination (whether you're sending the audience to your website or a page on LinkedIn), then it's time to create your ad
- The rules here are exactly the same as for Facebook: the picture matters as it's the element that will draw the visitor's eye. Then they'll scan the headline for a perceived benefit. Remember to be clear about benefits and what will happen when they click on the ad.
- Image size is 50x50px and it's important to add a picture as ads with an image are 20% more likely to be clicked on.
- The ad headline length is a maximum of 25 characters with the ad body allowing 75 characters.
- Once you've written your ad, you can click Duplicate to create a duplicate version, allowing you to test different image and/or copy. If you're undecided between 2 pictures, for example, you

can test the click through rates using each, thus allowing your audience to choose

Once you're done setting up your ad, click Next to move to the targeting options....

Targeting Your Audience

The targeting options available include:

- Geography: From targeting continents to specific cities, the geo targeting allows physical shops and businesses serving a specific location to keep their advertising costs economical.
- Company: you can target specific companies by name (useful for laser targeting high value potential clients) or companies by category (size or industry). If you know your audience really well, now you can target them precisely.
- Job Titles: Again, if you know who in your target customer' organisations is responsible for the buying decision, you can narrow your ad focus onto them using the job title targeting. There's no need to waste money advertising to lower level workers if it's upper level management who will be making a decision!
- Groups: you can choose which groups on LinkedIn you'd like to target. There are tens of thousands of groups on LinkedIn ranging from groups regarding a product development inside a company to a company's official group to post job openings etc. You might want to do some research on the groups you'd like to target

before adding them. It is a time consuming task but it narrows down your target audience effectively.

- Skills: For LinkedIn advertising, targeting by skills is almost the equivalent of targeting Facebook ads by interest. If your audience is primarily accountants, you can choose 'accountants' in the skills section to narrow your ad visbility to target only those who match your ideal customer.
- Gender and age targeting hopefully need little explanation!
- The last option 'also reach LinkedIn members on other websites through LinkedIn Audience Network' gives your ads legs outside the LinkedIn site. This checkbox gives permission for your ads to be shown on websites that are connected to LinkedIn or show LinkedIn content. If a user is signed up in their LinkedIn account while visiting one of those sites, they can see a personalised ad if they fall into your targeted audience criteria you just set.

So your ad and variations are set, your audience is targeted and it's time to get down to the money...

Budget and Billing

Ads on LinkedIn can get expensive quite quickly. Generally the Cost Per Click (CPC) is a multiple of what Facebook charges, probably due to the quality of the audience. But this means that keeping a close eye on budget is advisable, particularly with new and untested campaigns.

There are two payment options in LinkedIn:
- Pay-per-click (CPC): with this option, you specify the maximum amount of money you're willing to pay each time someone clicks on the ad. This option is a good bet if you're not sure how many people will click on the ad or what your conversion rate is, because you only pay for real ad clicks.
- Pay-per-1000 impressions (CPM): There are 2 scenarios when CPM is a good choice:
  a. When you want to 'spread awareness' and don't care too much about how many people click on the ad. This is similar to display advertising where you're paying for the visibility rather than the clicks themselves
  b. If you have a well-performing ad campaign and are generating a lot of clicks, it can sometimes work out cheaper to choose a CPM payment model if you can get more clicks per 1000 impressions than the industry average.
- You'll then get to set your daily budget, stopping you from being *too* liable should you forget to turn off the ads
- Minimum costs (in US Dollars. For local currency a rough conversion is done by LinkedIn):
  a. Minimum daily budget is $10/day.

    b. Minimum CPC bid is $2/click.

    c. Minimum CPM bid is $2/1000 impressions.

- If your ad campaign is seeking to generate high quality leads that you can follow up with by email, the Lead Collection option is a neat trick. This allows your audience to click on the ad to agree to share their contact details with you. You're then notified by email that they've shared their details with you and you can contact them by email or through LinkedIn to tell them more about your business or service.
- There's a starting fee associated with launching a LinkedIn ad campaign of $5 (again, roughly converted to local currency) that becomes an ad credit once the campaign is live.

Social Media Tools - The good, the bad and the paid

Unless you're a professional full time social media marketer, keeping each of your social profiles up-to-date, posting content and responding to interactions might seem like a completely unrealistic goal. Your time is valuable - too valuable to waste - and that's why wherever possible we recommend using tools to shortcut and simplify your social media marketing.

In this section we'll take a look at some of the most common social media management tools that allow you to simply manage, track and analyse each of your platforms from one place. Whether it's saving you from distractions by timing posts to drip feed during the week, notifying you of incoming direct messages or monitoring audience size over time, these tools are here to make your life *significantly* easier.

They bring a sense of order to the chaos and present your entire social world in a more easy-to-digest dashboard. We'll be looking at each of their pros and cons and which aspects of a social media marketing campaign they're best suited to.

Tweetdeck

Tweetdeck is a really neat tool for managing Twitter accounts simply and easily. It's so good in fact, that Twitter bought it, making it even better by giving it preferential treatment and access to its API.

Pros:
- You can sign in on multiple accounts and view each timeline at once without having to switch views (desktop app feature). If you've got different company divisions with separate Twitter accounts, businesses and personal accounts or you manage a number of clients, being able to see multiple feeds in one window is a huge timesaver.
- Tweetdeck allows you to set up customised columns with filters like hashtags, lists, searches or particular handles (like your competitors, perhaps). This means you can be constantly monitoring things of interest to you, whether it's people tweeting your competitors complaining about poor service, people mentioning your name (not Twitter handle) or people mentioning a specific problem that you can solve for them. Again, having all of this visible in one window without having to create a new search each time is a huge timesaver.
- Tweet scheduling: Rather than typing and sending tweets in real time, Tweetdeck's scheduling functionality allows you to schedule pre-written tweets and set the time you'd like

them to be sent. Particularly useful for people managing accounts with a time difference or for businesses whose customers are most active outside business hours, now you can be in front of your audience when *they're* ready.

- One of the best features about Tweetdeck is the ability to bypass Twitter's famous 140 characters limit. You can type a longer tweet and Tweetdeck will automatically shorten it up for you, creating a link that, when clicked, will lead the reader to a page containing the full tweet. Some say this defeats the point of Twitter, but for those of us who are not blessed with brevity it's an absolute lifesaver!
- Customisable themes allow you to modify the look of the dashboard
- In addition to Twitter, Tweetdeck can be setup to monitor your Facebook, Foursquare, LinkedIn, and MySpace profiles as well
- You can also post on the Facebook pages you manage directly via Tweetdeck.
- Manage basic Twitter activities like following, unfollowing, blocking, and reporting people/tweets using Tweetdeck, all from the same dashboard that you monitor your feed from.
- Customised alerts notify you with a sound whenever someone mentions you in their tweet or a ping whenever you receive a direct message (don't worry - you can turn this feature off as well).

- Tweetdeck also has a Google Chrome extension as well, meaning you don't have to download the desktop app.
- Mobile apps for iOS, Android, and Windows 7 platforms allow you to take Tweetdeck with you wherever you go.

Cons:

- It is bulky. Those cool layout features make it a fairly heavy piece of software. Although most modern PCs will have no trouble running it, if speed is an issue with more processor intensive apps for you then this might be worth bearing in mind.
- The horizontal layout has its limit. Showing so much information on one screen can make it hard to manage if you have lots of windows opened in Tweetdeck. Obviously it gets even harder when moved to a smaller smartphone screen.
- Although you can post on Facebook via Tweetdeck, you can't manage individual Facebook pages for comments, posts, interactions and so on, meaning that you still have to visit the page in question.
- Probably the biggest and most notable flaw in Tweetdeck is its inability to produce analytics.

Hootsuite

Hootsuite is another very cool social media management tool that can be used to manage multiple social media accounts across different platforms. The tool of choice at Exposure Ninja, it's one of the most popular choices out there amongst those

Pros:
- It comes with free, pro, and enterprise licensing options.
- You can use it to manage Twitter, Facebook, LinkedIn, WordPress, Google Plus, and Foursquare.
- It too has the ability to schedule updates (tweets, Facebook posts), including posting across all your networks at a set time.
- Collaboration options allow you to work as a team and delegate replies and other tasks
- It provides very insightful and customised analytics, good enough to present to management or clients without much additional work
- Mobile apps for Android, iOS, and BlackBerry although there is no app for Microsoft Windows Phone.

Cons:
- One of the most frustrating omissions is the ability to see who has retweeted you on Twitter.
- Although the app is marketed as free, the features in the free version are quite limited.

- The analytics is one component that isn't available in the free version. Detailed analytics can be expensive; as low as $50 and as high as $500 per report.
- You are restricted to the ow.ly URL shortener. For most this isn't a problem, but if you have your own short URL or use another service for the analytics, Hootsuite probably isn't for you.
- If you've enabled bulk status updates or the option to update Facebook from RSS feeds, thumbnail images don't appear in the posts, meaning that you miss out on that extra Edge weight and having a picture stand out and catch your audience's eye.
- The collaborative teams feature, while very neat, is relatively expensive.

Buffer

Buffer or Bufferapp, is a relatively new player in the social media management market although it boasts over a million of users already. While it offers browser versions, many of its users use this app on their smartphones instead of the web version. Let's take a look at the good and the bad of Buffer.

Pros:

- As the name suggests, the main purpose of Buffer is to let you save tweets and posts and have them uploaded at a scheduled time.
- It works works with Twitter, Facebook, LinkedIn (including LinkedIn company pages), and now Google+.
- It's available free of charge
- The free version allows you to sign in using two profiles
- The Buffer browser extension lets you tweet any website you've currently opened in a tab. Just click on the extension icon and it will save the tweet, timing it to go out according to your pre-defined schedule.
- You can use your own URL shortening service.
- The web interface is easy to use.
- The paid plans offer a discount for yearly signups.

Cons:

- The free account only allows ten posts on a given day and only from two accounts at a time.

ProPlanner

ProPlanner is only targeted towards Facebook. So, if you're just warming up to the idea of having a Facebook page for your business, ProPlanner suits you.

Pros:
- Variety of features and tools differing from sort of a jack-of-all social media tools.
- You can not only add Facebook pages but also groups to be managed.
- You can put the pages/links in lists and post a single post to multiple pages in a few clicks.
- Scheduled posts.
- Customized images to go along with every post. That's very cool.
- Both free and pro edition. Free is quite all right for basic purposes.
- Cool features such as status ideas, fresh content etc. I have personally used Post Planner and am a big fan of its status ideas feature.
- You can use it for as many Facebook pages as you want.
- Team collaboration.

Cons:
- The license costs from $4.95 to $24.95 a month, depending on the features that come with it.
- Only available for Facebook.

The Verdict

We've had a brief look at some of the most popular social media management tools, but as you might imagine this is only scratching the surface as there are dozens of others each with their own advantages and disadvantages.

Every business is different, and the tool that will best suit you depends on what you need it for. Our suggestion is to pick a couple to try out. Once you've got your accounts set up and had a play with the interface you'll soon discover what you do and don't like about them. To help you decide, here are some considerations:

- If you're a small business or have a very low budget, then your priority might be to find a tool that offers a free version that fulfills your requirements. We often assume that paid means better, when actually the features available in Tweetdeck, for example, are enough for most small and medium sized businesses.
- Consider the social media networks you actually use: if you only use Twitter and Facebook, with LinkedIn occasionally, then opting for a tool that covers many other social media platforms isn't necessarily a wise idea if it's going to cost you a little extra or come at the expense of tighter integration with the platforms you're using.

- If you don't need fancy features like team collaboration, don't go for tools that offer them and charge you money for them.
- Analytics are very useful but they can easily get expensive, too. Only opt for this features if your company's social media budget allows you to, and if standard Google analytics and URL shortener analytics aren't enough to give you the metrics you need.

If you want our simple recommendation, it's this: try Tweetdeck and if you need more functionality have a go with Hootsuite.

Listening

Although much of the time spent on social media marketing focusses on *talking* and pushing out your message (because that is what drives your audience), it goes without saying that listening has a really important role to play in good social strategy. The opportunity to listen to existing conversations going on around the world on social networks is one of the most exciting aspects, and very few people take full advantage. Those that do often limit their listening to mentions of their brand or company name which, if they are a small or medium-sized business, are few and far between.

In this section we're going to explore listening at a deeper level. We'll explore its use as a method of attracting new customers and generating leads through a process we call Outbound Social Lead Generation (OSLG) and show how you can directly profit from your competitor's mistakes (and lack of listening!).

The approach that is talked about in many social media marketing books and courses is naturally suited to large companies that already attract a lot of social media discussion. They'll advise you to listen out for mentions of your brand name, and try to settle any public customer service disputes quickly. This is, of course, great (if obvious) advice. But what does the local cake shop, plumber or accountant do when they only get a few mentions per week - or less - on Twitter, and mostly from people they already know?

The truth is that listening out for mentions of your own business is only the starting point. In this chapter we'll be exploring how those businesses that aren't yet receiving a lot of inbound tweets and Facebook posts can use existing conversations to grow their customer base.

The opportunity that social media gives us to listen in on millions of conversations taking place around the world in different niches is completely unprecedented. Marketers and business owners living in a time where this sort of real world feedback was only available through expensive research or DIY surveying would be blown away by the market intelligence available to all of us, free of charge, at any time of day or night. We can now get a real-life glimpse inside practically any industry in just a few clicks: what are your customers saying to each other? How are your competitors responding to communications from their customers? Which groups are vocal and which groups are invisible? Are people complaining about something and are these complaints are going unanswered?

There's a staggering amount of data out there and one of the problems is knowing where to start. We'll begin with customer service, as it's an area you really can't ignore, no matter how minimal your social media involvement.

Customer Service & Handling Complaints

Any talk of listening on Social Media would not be complete without a look at customer service. Many larger companies are understandably intimidated by the scale of the social media customer service challenge they face. Rather than moan to their friends when they are overcharged in their latest phone bill, people can now head straight to Twitter and start moaning to their followers with a quick tweet or two. Where previously the phone company would hear about the problem and have a chance to rectify it *before* the customer complained publicly, now this pattern is reversed. The complaint is immediately presented to the wider world for anyone to see. By the time the phone company is aware of the problem, the complainant's followers have already likely judged them guilty and allowed the incident to affect their perception. If the complainer is an serious influencer, they might have a lot of followers and this complaint might have a real effect.

To make matters worse, these complainers never sleep. They're tweeting away all day every day and they don't care if it's during a holiday when the company customer service team aren't at their desks. The complainers expect help, NOW or they'll continue to moan.

It's a huge challenge and so far, large companies are addressing it in one of 2 ways:

1. By ignoring it. They bury their heads in the sand and their customers continue to discuss their

products and services in negative ways online, in full view of the general public and other potential customers.

2. By putting together a team of Twitter customer service agents, armed with the power to look into problems and produce solutions quickly. In the short term it might be the more expensive of the two, but long term it means increased satisfaction amongst their customers

Ignorance is not the basis of smart business strategy, and option 1 is a very short sighted and hopeful plan. Assuming that Twitter and the like will go away and that social media is a phenomenon not likely to last more than a few years sounds awfully like what some now ex-companies said during periods of technological disruption in the past. The Internet and e-commerce in particular offer some chilling lessons to companies who choose not to move with the times and embrace a world which is constantly changing to make the customer's life more convenient.

So clearly any company that values their reputation will seek to address social media complaints as swiftly as possible, even more so when they are public. But as someone reading a book on social media marketing, you don't need to be told that! Without further ado, then, here are some important guidelines to operate by when it comes to social media customer service:

Don't be afraid to say "sorry"

Your legal advice might tell you never to admit guilt and to wait until you have all the facts before agreeing who is to blame. But since when was it a good idea to give lawyers control of customer service?

Sometimes all a dissatisfied person wants is to vent their frustration and feel like they are being listened to. A simple message that says "sorry you've had a bad experience" and offers a first step towards resolution is often enough to diffuse the complaint entirely. More than just letting them know you've heard the complaint, a genuine human apology shows that a real person is on the other end of that Twitter handle, and - as strange as it might seem - that gives the complainer a different perspective to imagining their fight taking place against a huge faceless corporation that just doesn't care.

Take the discussion private

The next step is to take whatever conversation that started publicly, private. Usually this is done on Twitter by publicly asking the complainer a direct message with more information, in order for you to be able to handle the enquiry. This serves three main purposes:

1. It removes the argument from public eyes, thus removing the soapbox the complainer was standing on. Removing the audience also removes the complainant's power, and they'll often respond to this powerplay by doing absolutely nothing; the complaint dies there and then (although the dissatisfaction lingers...)

2. The privacy allows sharing of sensitive customer information so the problem can be addressed properly.
3. It puts the onus on the complainant. *They* now have to act. Whether it's following the brand and sending a Direct Message with customer service numbers or transaction IDs, this requires more effort than simply writing a tweet moaning about a perceived injustice. For many complaints, this effort is too much and the complaint diffuses there and then.

Stay strong but don't be aggressive

Although it's not a good idea to *avoid* apologising or admitting fault, it's important that your brand keeps its integrity. Publicly commenting on particular cases or mentioning specific team members is generally unnecessary in public and has the potential to damage your reputation, as well as the morale of any team members mentioned. Like the martial arts principle of Jū, you want to accept your opponents attack and use it to your advantage rather than stand rigidly and take a punch to the face. So instead of dwelling on the problem or getting too caught up in apportioning blame, focus on finding a solution that makes everyone happy.

On the other hand, showing aggression or defiance in complaint responses is a recipe for disaster, and things can quickly get out of hand. In a recent episode of TV show Kitchen Nightmares featuring fiery chef Gordon Ramsay, an Arizona restaurant called Amy's Baking Company failed to capitalise on the good publicity a nationwide TV appearance *should* have caused, and instead began one of the most horrifying (yet entertaining) social media meltdowns in history.

Their Facebook page (https://www.facebook.com/amysbakingco) was targeted by viewers who started leaving comments about the show and the owner Amy. Amy and the team responded with aggression, which in turn attracted more attention. As the page began to go viral on social sharing site Reddit, more and more people began leaving comments not just about the show and staff, but how they were handling the rapidly accelerating runaway train. This in turn produced even more aggressive responses from the page owners who by now had started a full scale meltdown:

"I AM WONDER WOMAN. I AM A GREAT CHEF, A GREAT WIFE, AND A GREAT MOM TO MY KIDS. AND WE WILL BE PARENTS TO A HUMAN KID, ONE DAY TO. WE WILL SHOW ALL OF YOU."

"WE ARE NOT FREAKING OUT. WE DO NOT CARE ABOUT A "WITCH HUNT" I AM NOT A WITCH. I AM GODS CHILD. P*** OFF ALL OF YOU. F*** REDDITS, F*** YELP AND F*** ALL OF YOU. BRING IT. WE WILL FIGHT BACK."

Nothing says 'calm and controlled' like caps lock, right? For those who enjoy that sort of thing the Facebook page is well worth a visit.

Clearly this is an extreme case, but cases like this prove that meeting hostility with aggression just doesn't work online. Once situations get emotional, they have the potential to quickly get out of control. It's interesting to see how quickly the online community gathered like sharks as soon as there was blood in the water. The takeaway is no matter how personal the issue feels, try to never respond in an emotional way.

Almost every business will, at some point, have dissatisfied customers. Even if it's through no fault of their own, it's just a part of doing business and serving a lot of people. When the comments come, it's important to learn from them and meet them in a respectful and appreciative way.

Measuring Influence

The truth is that not all of your followers and fans are equally important to you. Endorsement from your most influential followers can be worth a lot more to your bottom line than happy tweets from a regular Joe. These influencers tend to have a larger audience and more influence with that audience. If you can turn them into raving fans for your business, they'll do the promotion for you. How can you identify who in your audience is most influential online?

Klout aims to bring the measurement of influence to social media. Your Klout score is a number from 1-100 based on your relationship with your followers, the engagement of your updates and the topics on which you are considered an influencer. For example, if you regularly tweet out content that gets shared, replied to and favourited, your Klout score will be higher than someone whose tweets get no reaction. If your Facebook posts get a lot of likes, comments and shares, you'll have more 'Klout' than someone with few friends who rarely uses it. Klout measures and combines influence on each of your social networks to give you one overall score.

While a single algorithm might not be able to measure influence 100% accurately, Klout is a pretty good indicator and does a neat job of representing something so complex in a simple to understand single number. As the next generation of web content becomes deeply connected to authorship and the authority of the author, it will be interesting to see how Klout develops.

Those who have a high Klout score are offered 'Perks'. These can be anything from discounts to free gifts, advance product previews and screenings of movies to extra services when staying at certain hotels. Brands partner with Klout to offer these perks with the hope that the influencers who receive them will be so impressed that they decide to tell their following about the experience. It's a strategy that has proven popular with brands: in May 2013 Klout delivered its 1 millionth perk.

It's important to remember that this is still early days for Klout, and in its first three years much has been made of the potential uses for Klout scores, from influencing hiring decisions to affecting loan availability (the theory goes that influential people are more likely to be financially stable). While much of this is purely theoretical, I think we can expect to see online influence measurements having a greater and greater effect on 'real life' as they become more accurate. With enough data, patterns will begin to emerge between influence and things like financial status and marketing potential. Influence score is one more statistic that allows us to quantify things that previously required manual analysis, and that's what the Internet is so expert at doing.

So what about taking Klout into consideration in your social media marketing?

The Klout plugin for Google's Chrome browser displays Twitter users' Klout scores next to their profile pictures when you use the Twitter web interface, which is really useful when you're browsing, checking @replies and doing outreach to influential people in your market.

With this indication of influence you'll be able to prioritise your time and energy on the most important contacts and those with the potential to spread your message furthest.

Of course all this talk of prioritising influential people doesn't mean that you should neglect those with low Klout scores or treat your less influential followers like irrelevant outcasts; they might simply have not set up their Klout account properly or be in the habit of creating share worthy content yet. Today's low Klout scorers might be tomorrow's influencers, so relationships that you make with them now could lead to much greater exposure for you in the future. It really depends how much time and energy you have to dedicate to your social outreach, and Klout score is just one more metric for helping you make informed decisions.

Social Media For Lead Generation

The potential for using social media to bring you highly qualified fresh leads is really exciting. What's more, unlike forms of advertising where a potential customer has to actively search for a solution to their problem in order to be shown an ad, social media gives you the ability to reach out to people who are complaining and present a solution, *without them having to do any of the work*. We can be right there at the point of pain, offering a targeted solution.

In the sections covering advertising we look at targeting people according to *their likes and interests*, but the strategies we're covering in this section are even more focussed and can bring an unbelievable response rate. They involve a little more work than set-and-forget adverts, but with the right offer and sales process they can be extremely profitable.

OSLG (Outbound Social Lead Generation)

OSLG is particularly exciting for businesses that solve a problem, particularly in a local market. Because it's new, this sort of strategy is very unlikely to be on your competitors' radars. People tend to spend money on advertising that is sold by someone, whether it's local newspapers, yellow pages or Google Adwords. OSLG isn't sold by anyone on a large scale (yet), so it's just not part of their consciousness.

The principle of Outbound Social Lead Generation is this: people are in your area complaining about problems that your product or service solves. By offer help, advice or a targeted offer over social media, you can be in their consciousness right at the point when they need you most. For example:

"They say it comes in 3's first a broken dryer then my boiler packed up again now a burst water pipe in my bathroom! #VERYANNOYED" @Suzie (Twitter handle disguised)

This tweet got no responses from plumbers, despite the fact that there are plenty of them in Suzie's city, and many are paying an average £2.30 per click on Google Adwords to reach people with plumbing problems. Here is a potential customer crying for help and no one came to the rescue.

Searching for locally relevant tweets used to require third party apps and plenty of hassle, but it's now easier than ever thanks to Twitter's own advanced search. In the example above, all any of the plumbers in Newcastle upon Tyne would have to do is search for:

boiler near:"Newcastle upon tyne" within:10mi

This tells Twitter to find tweets using the word 'boiler' within 10 miles of Newcastle-upon-Tyne. It's simple and if they're monitoring this search they'll be seeing jobs pop up that their competitors would have no idea about. While they might not be getting 3 jobs per day from this strategy, it's free and can be set up to take no time at all.

But perhaps the plumber doesn't only want to find boiler jobs?

boiler OR plumber OR drainage OR blocked drain OR central heating OR radiator near:"Newcastle upon tyne" within:10mi

If they want to get really fancy and narrow the search to tweets that have negative intent and include a question, they can search:

boiler OR plumber OR drainage OR blocked drain OR central heating OR radiator near:"Newcastle upon tyne" within:10mi :(?

And so on. The list of Twitter search operators is extensive (see below) and how you use them will depend on your specific market and your audience.

Once you've identified a search that works for your market and brings up relevant tweets, you can save it. This allows you to access it quickly in future from a Twitter app on your computer or phone. Using an application like Tweetdeck can give you the option to keep this search open at all times, seeing live updates

Operator	Finds tweets...
twitter search	containing both "twitter" and "search". This is the default operator.
"happy hour"	containing the exact phrase "happy hour".
love OR hate	containing either "love" or "hate" (or both).
beer -root	containing "beer" but not "root".
#haiku	containing the hashtag "haiku".
from:alexiskold	sent from person "alexiskold".
to:techcrunch	sent to person "techcrunch".
@mashable	referencing person "mashable".
"happy hour" near:"san francisco"	containing the exact phrase "happy hour" and sent near "san francisco".
near:NYC within:15mi	sent within 15 miles of "NYC".
superhero since:2010-12-27	containing "superhero" and sent since date "2010-12-27" (year-month-day).
ftw until:2010-12-27	containing "ftw" and sent up to date "2010-12-27".
movie -scary :)	containing "movie", but not "scary", and with a positive attitude.
flight :(	containing "flight" and with a negative attitude.
traffic ?	containing "traffic" and asking a question.

hilarious filter:links	containing "hilarious" and linking to URLs.
news source:twitterfeed	containing "news" and entered via TwitterFeed

Twitter search operators. Source: twitter.com

as new tweets matching your search criteria come in. Alerts can be configured meaning that you find out as soon as someone posts a tweet matching your criteria.

If you want to identify your own OSLG target customer, here are some questions to ask:

- How might you identify people who in need of your product or service?
- Do they buy something else around the same time that they need you? For example personal trainers can strike when the iron is hot by congratulating and offering tips to those tweeting about joining a gym or checking in for the first time.
- Are your customers at a certain place in life when they need your service? For example local furniture stores could send tweets welcoming
- people to the area and offering a 'welcome free gift' if they tweet or post updates about moving into a new house or apartment and are located within 10 miles. Wedding venues can send congratulatory tweets to people within a 40 mile radius posting statuses, tweets or pictures about

getting engaged. As can wedding photographers, catering companies, wedding planners etc. All of these service categories will, at some point, be required by the tweeter, so how better to introduce yourself than offer a simple

- congratulations and a free gift? It's still so unusual that you are very likely to get noticed.

This part requires your creativity as well as a little experimentation, both in your targeting and your approach. As cliched as it is, 'thinking outside the box' here can really help position you in a completely different way to your competitors, who are stuck standing in their shops hoping and praying that someone walks in needing what they offer.

Making the Sale

It's one thing to see tweets from people complaining about a problem that you can solve, but how do you make the sale?

The important thing to remember is that the person tweeting was not asking for business solicitations, nor are they expecting it. By bursting in and immediately pitching your service you're not going to be making friends *or* sales. As with all social media marketing, the best approach is to offer value first. Just letting someone in distress know that you've heard their cry and are here to help them if they need you is a good first step to building rapport.

If you're able to offer some specific advice which could help them partially (or even completely) solve their problem, you should take that opportunity as well. Remember your goal for social media is to build long-term awareness and create a community of potential customers who understand your value and consider you an authority. Even if that means offering advice to someone rather than straight up pitching them, you should take that opportunity because of what it could lead to in future.

If a helpful and polite plumber replied to @Suzie above giving some tips for stopping the water leak, limiting damage to her bathroom and offering to come and take a look immediately free of charge, that's going to be a tough series of tweets to ignore. If the tone is helpful and sympathetic rather than coming across like a shark smelling blood, the potential customer's first impression of the plumber is of someone that wants to help.

By taking the time out of their day and offering value (the tips) the plumber is demonstrating a willingness to help beyond just pitching their service. If @Suzie has already found someone to fix the solution, the Twitter plumber is still providing useful advice (how to limit damage) and @Suzie is likely to say thank you, at which point the plumber says "not to worry, if you need any help in future just tweet us!" and clicks to follow her.

@Suzie likes the sound of this help, feels a duty to reciprocate the kind tweets and the follow so decides to follow the plumber back. Target engaged.

@Suzie is now in the plumber's herd and by providing *interesting* and *useful* tweets in future (not things like "Watching the football" or "Stuck in traffic today") the plumber can begin to establish himself on Suzie's radar. Next time there's a leak, who is @Suzie going to call (or tweet)?

As well as offering original content to help someone, you can also direct them to other content on the net that solves their problem. While sending them somewhere else might initially seem counter-intuitive, it actually positions you as a knowledgeable expert who thinks beyond their own gain, and just wants to help.

If your potential customers tend to face a similar set of problems, you can put together a quick FAQ section on your website. Then, next time someone complains about facing one of these problems, a simple message offering sympathy and a link to the page containing the solution is all you need to position yourself and begin the relationship.

As you can see, Outbound Social Lead Generation is miles away from what most businesses are using social media for. This makes resistance extremely low amongst targets of such a campaign, as they are not yet tuning this sort of social outreach out. Your advertising can fly under their radar, because after all - if it looks like a friendly tweet and smells like a friendly tweet, it must just be a friendly tweet, right?

Straightforward Business Solicitations

While in my searches, I came across the following tweet which illustrates perfectly the type of situation where a business needs to pitch their offering in one tweet:

Please can anybody recommend a #plumber in the #lichfield area as #boiler has packed up @thisisLichfield @LichfieldLive @LichfieldBlog

How might you approach this sort of situation?

Time is of the essence here. You need to be the first on the scene with a compelling tweet and a strong call to action in order to get your foot in the door before anybody else. Although this tweeter is looking for someone to fix their boiler, what they're really asking for is recommendations. This shows that social proof and personal recommendation are important to them, and can be considered one of their primary sales triggers.

Armed with information about the problem and a clear idea for how they make buying decisions, you can create a well-crafted proposition which matches them closely. It has to be brief to fit in Twitter's 140 character limit, so there's no room for messing around. The format should be:

- Clear relevant benefit
- Strong call to action

In this case a clear relevant benefit could be the number of personal recommendations: "95% of our customers refer us to friends", "we're the most shared plumber in your town", or even just "most of our work comes from word-of-mouth". If actual twitter users can be included in the tweet ("@tony called about our emergency boiler repair "best service from a plumber ever"), so much the better. If you need more space, consider using one tweet for the benefit statement and one for the follow-up call to action.

For the call to action, we want to be strong and compelling but also offer something low risk and relatively low commitment. "Call us now" is NEVER a strong enough call to action on its own, because it doesn't answer any of the customer's questions, and leaves a considerable amount of doubt about what will happen next. Offer something that is difficult to turn down, whether it's a free gift for enquiring, free no obligation inspection or something else that involves very little risk for them with a large potential reward.

In the specific case above, my recommendation would be to offer a free inspection and prescription for the repair. It should be emphasised that this inspection comes with no obligation, and no hard sales pitch will be made (though of course a clear explanation of the problem and the cost to fix the problem will be outlined, and at that point the job is likely to be agreed).

If offering some sort of low commitment offer on the front end isn't viable, consider offer a new customer discount or free gift with first purchase in order to motivate people to act. If your profit-per-transaction is high, or your customers have a high 'lifetime value' then you can obviously afford to do more than a business with a very low cost-per-transaction or who sells one-off or infrequent purchases.

Knowing what you can afford to spend to attract each new lead requires that you understand some of your business's fundamental numbers:

- How much you are willing to spend to attract each new customer. If your average transaction size generates £100 profit, you might decide you are willing to spend £50 to generate each new sale.
- What your conversion rate is from leads to customers. For example if you know that on average 1 in every 3 new leads ends up buying from you, your conversion rate is ⅓ or 33%. You then know that you'll need to bring in 3 new leads each time you want 1 new customer
- Cost per lead. This is how much you can spend on each lead. If you are willing to spend £50 on acquiring a new customer and you convert 1 in 3

leads, you now know that you can spend £50/3 = £16.66 on attracting each lead. A free £15 shopping voucher just for enquiring is viable under these conditions.

Of course, the more tempting you make your 'bait' or free gift, the more unqualified leads you might attract, so it's important to keep re-evaluating your cost per lead and cost per customer.

Capitalising On Your Competitors' Mistakes

Because of the amount of social media marketing incompetence out there, capitalising on the mistakes of others in your industry can offer some easy pickings. Luckily people *love* to complain on social media. When we've had a bad experience with a particular company, complaining in public can feel extremely satisfying as our voice is finally being heard. We've covered how to deal with this for your own business elsewhere, but in this section we'll look at some different approaches you can take to capitalise on your competitors' inability to deal with customer complaints.

This strategy can work particularly well for businesses that pride themselves on offering a higher level of customer service than more established competitors, but really any business can take advantage of their rivals' inability to keep all of their customers happy.

In order to be there just at the right moment, you'll want to monitor mentions of your competitors and any relevant brand or product names. Each time somebody mentions that they're having a problem with your competitor, you send a sympathetic tweet or post apologising for the problem. That's it - you don't need to pitch them or explain why your service is better. Remember the reason most people vent their anger on social media is because they want to feel that they're being *listened to* and that the company responsible has recognised their problem. Sometimes a solution isn't possible or practical, but just the fact that they have had their complaint heard is enough to improve their mood. They are not necessarily in the right frame of mind to be pitched at, and might not be in a position to buy, so pitching your service is unnecessary and changes the vibe of your message from 'nice' to 'advert'.

But your offer of sympathy puts you on their radar. If they *are* unhappy and ready to buy, then you are there right when they need you and you've differentiated yourself from the others in your market by showing that you care. They can investigate further and will be intrigued to see why you've responded to their tweet when often the company they are moaning about hasn't. They'll likely check your profile, your other recent tweets (to see if you do this sort of thing a lot), and will visit your website if it's linked from your profile.

Clearly, the more influential the complainant, the more effective this strategy can be at generating shares, RTs and other coverage.

Demonstrating your Expertise

Many businesses underestimate the value of the expertise contained within their team. Even if you are relatively new in your field, the fact that you spend your time specialising in something gives you expertise over and above your customers.

Say for example you're a hair stylist working straight out of college, there are dozens/hundreds/thousands of potential clients in your area who would appreciate an honest opinion on what sort of hairstyle might suit them. If you're a wedding photographer, offering 5 tips to judge a good wedding photographer from a bad one would be extremely useful for the hundreds of brides and grooms nearby who pay for wedding photography each year without really knowing what they should be looking for.

What sort of expertise is present in your business, and who would benefit from it? Just like the other listening strategies we've discussed, demonstrating your expertise is a great opportunity to put yourself in front of people who have identified themselves as potential future customers and position yourself as an authority who cares.

Whether you create a formalised process for demonstrating your expertise (offering audits, quotes or consultations) or you just get into the habit of answering questions people write you on your blog or through social media, being able to demonstrate your expertise in public can give you a real 'authority' persona on social media. Holding Q&A sessions, Google+ hangouts, writing and promoting blog posts that answer some of the most common questions or making videos explaining your answers can all lead to shares, RTs and wider publicity in your industry. Of course none of this happens overnight and it requires a level of commitment, especially in the early days when there will be more As than Qs.

Social Media and SEO

Because of our background as an SEO company, we can't resist talking about the impact that a good social media campaign can have on your search engine visibility. SEO is approaching a very exciting period whereby not just the content but also the *author* of the content has an effect on its exposure. As we've seen earlier in the book, Google+ in particular is a social channel that is *already* affecting the SEO world in a big way. We rarely embark on an SEO campaign that doesn't include Google+ strategies because they are simply too effective to ignore.

Author Rank

There has been much speculation about how Google will use information about a blog post or website's author's authority. Following the introduction of Google+ Authorship in 2011, mention was made by a Google engineer who speculated that Google could use some sort of authority measurement to impact ranking. Then somebody uncovered some patents Google had filed along those lines, and the concept of Author Rank began to grow some pretty big and powerful legs.

So what is the idea behind Author Rank, and how can we use it?

Currently there is a lot of information on the web that is anonymous. From Google's perspective, they also see that most spam and low quality content is anonymous, whilst the content that is publicly attributed to an author tends to be better quality and more valuable, for example public blog posts written by industry experts. This isn't to say that all anonymous content will be identified as SPAM, but if for example Google is trying to decide which of two articles to rank highest for a particular phrase. One is anonymous whilst the other is written by a published author, influential in their field and with active social profiles where they talk to other authorities in their area of expertise and have their content shared.

If you had to bet on one or the other article being most useful to searchers, you might conclude that the article written by the established authority would win, and thus it should rank higher. This is the essence of the concept behind Author Rank.

It's our opinion that in the future of the web, authorship will become as important in online search as it is in 'real' life. That is, Google will seek to mimic the analysis we do of authority figures when showing search results. We trust a qualified doctor working in a well known surgery more than someone off the street, so why wouldn't this be useful in deciding which websites should be highest visibility? This fits perfectly with their pattern of seeking to incorporate real life quality and popularity signals into their algorithms.

So that's the future. How do we take advantage of this now? The world of authorship is already here with Google+ authorship. Using authorship markup with your website content allows your picture to be displayed in search results. We've found that simply having this picture displayed boosts click through rate on the search results pages *significantly*, and sites with Authorship markup ranking 2nd or 3rd can often attract more traffic than an anonymous position 1 result.

To use Google authorship markup you first need to have an established Google+ personal profile with a clear headshot profile picture. You'll then need to add the URL of any sites or pages that your content appears on in the 'Contributor to' section of your Google+ profile.

Next, you'll want to add a link from this content back to your profile so that people on your site can find your Google+ profile. Do this using the following code, substituting in your own profile link:

<a href="https://plus.google.com/109412257237874861202?rel=author">Google</a>

Alternatively you can visit https://plus.google.com/authorship and submit an email address matching the domain name, although we've found this method to take longer and be less reliable than linking the content manually.

Not only does Google+ Authorship mean that your picture can show up in search results, but as we discussed in the Google+ chapter earler, it can also lead to higher rankings for people just outside your network of contacts. If a searcher is logged into their Google+ account at the time of searching (which many Google+ users are), search results that *their* contacts have +1'd are given preferential treatment in the results pages. E.g. my friend has 'liked' a particular page, so even though that site might not be ordinarily ranking on page 1 for this particular search, I see it on page 1 because Google has decided it is likely to be relevant to me personally. This is all part of Google's 'Search Plus Your World' or SPYW, which is designed to present results relevant to individual users based on their network of contacts. If you're looking for a restaurant to visit in your hometown, recommendations from certain friends hold more weight than recommendations from strangers because you have built up trust and are also familiar with their particular tastes. Search Plus Your World is an early incarnation of this principle applied online.

This sort of social media integration in search will become more and more prevalent as Google and Facebook discover new ways to tap into our *actual* social networks to show us personalised results. Of course fundamental to all of this new technology is that your business or website is extremely visible on whatever social network your audience uses, and that you have a good following and positive reviews to give your results more weight.

Content Freshness

For many of our SEO clients who don't have the time or inclination to keep their websites updated with fresh content, we embed social media (usually Twitter or Facebook feed) on the site itself, so when they tweet or post a status update, the site appears updated too. Not only does this show Google that something is going on and the site is alive and active, but it also shows website visitors that the business is alive and kicking.

This can also work in the reverse direction for website owners who are used to updating a blog, but aren't used to regularly update their social media profiles. In this case we'll set up an auto posting plugin so that when they create a new blog post, it's automatically posted from their social media accounts as well. This makes it really easy to keep all your social profiles looking active, and gives followers the same experience wherever they follow you.

To set this up from a Wordpress site, we use the SNAP (Social Networks Auto Poster) plugin which allows you to link Facebook, Twitter, Google+, LinkedIn, Pinterest, Tumblr and Blogger accounts, amongst others. It's a free plugin and dead simple to use.

Backlinks

Another significant SEO benefit for active social media profiles is backlink generation. It's becoming increasingly difficult to find good clean sources of backlinks thanks to Google's mission to clean up webspam, but social media is just such a source. The good news is that by following the strategies outlined in this book you'll be generating some excellent quality backlinks.

What are backlinks?
For those who are unfamiliar and haven't read our book How to Get to the Top of Google, backlinks are links to your website from elsewhere on the internet. The reason that they're important is because Google takes the number and quality of these backlinks into account when deciding where to rank websites in its search results. A website that has been tweeted about, shared on Facebook and has lots of other links from around the net is more likely to be considered an authority than a site which has no links and isn't mentioned on social media at all. It's just like being at school again: Google wants to pick the best players for its search results football team, and those tend to be the kids that everyone is talking about.

As long as you post links to any new website content you produce, you'll be creating backlinks. But you can turbocharge this strategy by creating content that other people will want to share, retweet and repost, thus generating even more backlinks from other people in your industry. In this way, good *SEO* social media strategy begins to look a lot like good *regular* social media strategy, which is kind of the point.

How can you turbocharge your social media for SEO and use it to generate more links?

The first thing to understand is that your content needs to be sharable. That is, interesting to your audience and gives them an answer to the question "'what's in it for me to share this?" Whether the answer is that it makes them look like an expert, it's funny & entertaining or it boosts their credibility (for example you write an article mentioning them), your audience will rarely share something just because they see the words "please share" or "please tweet". For specific strategies to build shareable content, please see the 'Creating Shareable Content' chapter.

The second element of a turbocharged social-media-for-SEO campaign is making sure the focus of your messages is on your own website. Your website needs to be your hub; the place where all the information is gathered that people can go to find out everything they need about your subject. Retweeting and posting links to other people's sites is all well and good, but those aren't directly helping your SEO. If you see an article that interests you, rather than just tweet the link, if you have time and are so inclined you can write a blog post about the article, giving your own take on the situation and perhaps adding some new ideas to the conversation. Of course you'd want to include a link to the original article in your blog post, but the point is that where possible you want to be promoting your own website and your own content rather than other people's.

Of course it's not realistic to expect you to write reaction articles on every little piece of news that surfaces in your industry, and sometimes for the sake of speed you might simply want to post content that other people have made. But from an SEO perspective if you are going to be posting something that will be shared or retweeted, best to make that link pointing at your own website wherever possible.

Creating Search-Optimised Social Media Profiles

As well as your social media *content* being potentially useful for SEO, your *profiles* themselves can also play their part. Anywhere you are given the opportunity to link to your website, obviously you'll want to take it. But don't forget that you can also include links in profile descriptions as well, where relevant.

Your Google+ page in particular can be an excellent way to link back to various places on your website. When talking about the results you get for your customers, you can link to your testimonials page for example; mentioning the areas you serve, if you are a local business, can include a link to your Service Areas page and so on.

The key is, just as with any SEO, to make your linking seem natural. There is no need to go crazy embedding links in every sentence, but for examples like the above where visitors to your profile page might actually find it useful to see a certain section on your website, a well-placed backlink or 3 certainly won't go amiss.

With Google+ in particular, you have the option to verify your website address using a couple of different methods. This step is important because non-verified pages won't show up as an expanded listing in Google search results, and Google+ users who find your profile won't see your website address in the About section. Your options for verifying your website address are as follows, in order of simplicity:

1. Click Verify, and if your site already has a linked Webmaster Tools account, log in and confirm that you want to allow the site to be linked to the Google+ page
2. Add the code supplied by Google to your website. We usually add it in the footer as this means it'll be visible on every page.

Measuring Social Media ROI

In the world of Social Media, many SMM companies view ROI (Return On Investment) as a bit of a dirty word. It's as if Pope Julius II was stood in the Sistine Chapel yelling up at Michelangelo asking the ROI on his ceiling painting, and the increase in tourist donations he could expect in the centuries to follow. But fine art social media isn't, and we believe it should be a business decision made just like any other - cost in vs profit out. Just because it has a bit of a soft and fluffy image doesn't mean it's not useful in a hard nosed business sense as well, as long as proper tracking is put in place.

It's true that there are a lot of untrackable benefits to social media. As an extension of word of mouth, the sort of brand awareness and familiarity that a good social media campaign can generate - not to mention individual customer service queries - can not always be quantified. But that doesn't prevent us from being fastidious about collecting data and measuring the effects of our work on traffic and sales as much as we can.

At the risk of sounding contradictory, we recommend almost *every single client* who gets in touch wanting to improve their website ranking starts using social media if they're not already; not because it will directly lead to sales for them, but because the SEO benefits are usually enough *on their own* to warrant an active or semi-active campaign. This is only set to increase as we move to the period of increased attribution and content ownership.

Different Tracking Scenarios

How you track your social media ROI will depend heavily on your website purpose and overall marketing plan. A purely e-commerce site will clearly require different tracking to a roofer's blog looking to generate phone calls, whilst a local business relying on in-person visits has their own set of tracking challenges altogether.

In the following section we'll go through different tracking techniques so you can pick and choose those that suit your particular business and match your technical capabilities.

First Touch vs Last Touch

One final point before we dive in is understanding the importance of a complete marketing funnel and where each of your marketing pieces (including social media) fits in. In tracking, this concepts of 'first touch' (the first time the user comes across your brand or a product) and 'last touch' (the final step that leads them to buy) are useful to understand the role that a variety of different pieces of the puzzle have, to make sure we're not over-crediting or under-crediting any single marketing piece. To illustrate, let's take an example:

Some of the readers of this book will claim the free Online Marketing audit offered at the beginning. They'll go to the Exposure Ninja website, fill in the form and receive a detailed audit with suggestions of how to boost their own social media profile and use it to grow their business. Once they've received this audit, many of them will ask us to implement this social media campaign for them. Some of them will talk to us on the phone, some will just use email.

So which piece of this marketing puzzle (the book, the website, the audit, phone conversation or the email follow up) do we attribute the sale to? For sure nothing would have happened without the book (first touch), but likewise without the phone conversation or email follow up (last touch) the sale wouldn't have happened. To make matters even more complicated, some of the readers of this book will have found us through referrals from other clients, social media, one of our other books, YouTube, footer links in websites that are outperforming theirs, magazine articles, interviews and so on. All this could happen before they even join the 'book - website - audit - followup - sale' path.

So while we can track either first touch (leads generated by social media) or last touch (sales/conversions directly resulting from social media messages) for your social media marketing campaign, it's important not to get too caught up in expecting each tweet to result in X sales, or worrying that you only have 300 followers and instead look at the big picture and combination of *all* your online marketing efforts.

Google Analytics for Social Media

Google Analytics gives us some fantastic measuring tools for social media, mostly around clicks, visitors and traffic. You can use it to see how many visitors are coming into your site from each network, how long they are staying, what they are reading while they are there and how many of them turn into customers, leads or other conversions. While an exhaustive explanation of all the features, uses and analysis available in Google Analytics is beyond the scope of this book, we'll take a look at the social media dashboard inside Google Analytics and understand some of the most useful social media specific features.

If you don't already have Google Analytics set up and installed on your website, head over to www.google.com/analytics and sign up. Once you've filled in your website's details you'll be given a piece of code which you or your website ninja will need to add to each page that you want to track (basically all of them, minus any 'hidden' pages). There's plenty of help available to set up Google Analytics online, and Google's own documentation is pretty good if you get stuck.

Once you've got Analytics up and running and you're starting to see some stats, like where your visitors are arriving on your site from (in the Traffic Sources section) we're ready to start getting a little more involved with the social aspect and setting up some **goals**.

Google Analytics goals are used to give an easily defined 'result' that we can use to measure the effectiveness of the promotion we do for your website. A goal can be many different things; signups, contact form submissions, clicking 'more' to see more information, a product purchase on an e-commerce website, playing a video, viewing contact information or becoming an affiliate. By defining and measuring these goals, not only can you track how effective your social media campaign is, you'll also be able to compare its effectiveness to other sources of traffic such as Google ads, organic search and direct traffic. This data can show you the *value* of your social media traffic. You might find that your traffic from Pinterest is a low percentage of all the visitors on your site but that these visitors tend to be better buyers than visitors from organic Google searches. Or vice versa. Whatever patterns you find, having the *data* means you can make informed decisions about where to focus your promotion.

Setting Up a Goal

To set up a goal for your site, go to Conversions in your Analytics dashboard, click goals and choose Overview. You'll see a button to Set up goals which will take you through the process of defining your goals. You can select a template from a list of sample goals, write a description and choose what sort of action defines the goal, for example landing on a thank you page after filling in a form or requesting more information. You can then define the goal in specific terms, for example choosing a destination URL that people visit once they have filled in a form on your site. You can also assign it a monetary value (if, for example, you know your average value per lead) as well as define any funnel that you have to lead people through the process of filling in the form or placing an order.

It's as simple as that! Once your goal is set up you can choose to verify it if you want to make sure it's 'wired up' properly, and then you're ready to start collecting data.

Because social media tends to generate links and traffic in a slightly different way to regular 'static' links, there is a special Social section inside the Google Analytics dashboard. Go to Traffic Sources / Social / Overview to get started. If you've set up a monetary value on your goals, this dashboard will show an estimate of you how much your social media traffic has been worth to you, broken down by Conversions, Contributed Social Conversions (conversions where social played a role anywhere along the path) and Last Interaction Social Conversions (conversions where social media was the 'last touch' sending the visitor to the site to buy).

You'll also be able to see the stats for each social network, helping you to identify which networks bring the most traffic as a percentage of total social traffic.

The Network Referrals tab gives more information about this, including how many pages visitors from each network visit on your site, as well as how long they stay. This can be quite an instructive statistic as it gives a glimpse into the relative quality of traffic from each network. These stats will be different according to your market and the content promoted on each network. For example one of our clients in home maintenance gets a small amount of traffic from video sites like YouTube and Dailymotion as a result of some promotional videos we made for them. While this traffic doesn't make up a large percentage of his *overall* traffic (organic search is by far the largest referrer), visitors from these video sites *are* extremely engaged, with their visits lasting an average of around 6 times as long as those who arrive from organic search. This tells us that for this particular service, video is an incredibly powerful tool. Those visitors who find the site through YouTube or Dailymotion (often through organic Google searches where they see these videos showing up in the search results) view on average between 2 and 6 times more pages per visit than those visitors who land on the site having seen something on Tumblr, Stumbleupon or Wordpress.

If your site suddenly starts getting an increase in traffic from social, checking the Landing Pages tab can help you to identify the content that is being shared, and on which social networks so you can focus more attention on promoting it. What we'll often see is that particular social networks respond well to certain types of content.

According to a July 2013 study by Gigya, Pinterest is responsible for 41% of all e-commerce traffic generated by social media, compared to 16% of all traffic overall. If you own an e-commerce website that gets a good amount of image shares of your products on Pinterest, this will come as no surprise to you. Neither will the fact that Pinterest traffic tends to convert at higher rates and spend more.

Using breakdowns of social traffic by page or by social network can really help you hone your social media campaign and put more resources into the sources already shown to be working and bringing you in leads.

Measuring Engagement with Social Plugins

If you're using Google +1, Facebook Like, Delicious Share and other social buttons, you can measure their engagement across your website to help you understand which posts, pages or other content is most popular. This allows you to feed the starving crowd more of what they want with the aim of generating more likes, shares and so on.

The installation of analytics for shares other than Google +1s (which are already tracked) is currently a lot more complicated than regular Analytics tracking and requires a level of technical expertise which is beyond the scope of this book, but Google has a guide here: https://developers.google.com/analytics/devguides/colle ction/analyticsjs/social-interactions

Feel free to contact us if you'd like help setting it up, otherwise our feeling is that someone will come up with a much simpler to use system to track content-specific likes from other networks within the next year or so.

What Else to Measure?

Clearly there are more metrics available in social media marketing than just sales, conversions and ROI. Audience size, engagement level, rate of new follower acquisition, follower profiles, Klout and so on all give us interesting feedback on how our social media marketing campaign is doing.

For Twitter at least rather than go through how each of these metrics is monitored, you can save time by using Followerwonk (www.followerwonk.com). It gives an unbeatable range of stats in both free and paid versions. For many the free version will be enough, although the paid version includes more advanced management: multiple accounts, downloading results in spreadsheet format and additional audience tracking and sorting (for example see how your follower count has changed over time).

One of the highlights of Followerwonk is the competitor analysis section which allows you to research any user's followers by location, gender, influence, number of tweets and even gets deep down into statistics like the percentage of their tweets which are retweets (indicating that they are highly engaged). This competitor analysis allows you to deconstruct your competitors' followings and find out how influential they *really* are.

Much of the statistics you might want to track on Facebook are provided by the excellent Page Insights included with every Facebook page.

From the Page Insights overview, you can see the number of page likers and your post reach, tracked over the previous 7 days, engagement level and detailed statistics about your previous 5 posts.

Clearly statistics like Post Reach (indicative of your Page's Edgerank) and engagement level are key when it comes to understanding how well your page is doing. Low interaction and post reach suggests that your posts aren't making it very far and are not achieving high visibility. There could be a number of reasons for this, but the most typical is that the posts themselves are not formulated to get a reaction from the audience. Whether they're too focused on your business rather than your customers, or they don't provide enough original value for your likers to engage, these are useful signs and can help you hone your strategy as you find the particular angle that will work best for you.

Under the Page Posts and People tabs you'll find even more information about everything from the ages of your audience to comparisons between the likes generated organically and those from paid ads. You can choose your own custom dates as well to monitor changes over time and around key events (like adding a Pinterest page or changing your profile picture.

Because there is so much to the new Facebook Insights dashboard, I really recommend going and having a play with what's available. If you're really short on time, here are my top 5 statistics to track:

1. Page Reach. This tells you how visible your page is on Facebook, which in turn indicates how much your audience have engaged with it in the past. The higher your Page Reach, the higher your Edgerank is (usually) so if you're more visible and likely to generate more interactions. It's a positive (or negative) feedback loop that starts with really engaging posts, so remember to put yourself in your audience's shoes and try to move yourself closer to their goals.

2. The All Posts table gives you excellent insight into your previous posts' performance from one place. You can use this big picture view to identify the angles and topics that work best for you with your audience.

3. The Posts / Best Post Types tab shows you which *types* of posts generate the best engagement for you. Whether it's posting links, re-posting tweets and statuses from other accounts, posting videos or photos or just simply updating your status, the table shows you average reach and engagement levels for your most common post types.

4. Page Likes. Yes it's a vanity number and gives no indication as to the effectiveness of your Facebook campaign, but it does impact your

visibility and can offer reassurance that you're going in the right direction, even if it feels slow at first.

5. When your fans are online. This is really important data as it allows you to get in front of your audience when they're most likely to see your posts. In addition to the times your audience is most active you'll also see the relative activity levels according to day. If you have a large Facebook audience and want to time a big news story, product release or special promotion, you can make an accurate decision based on your audience's activity rather than guesswork.

Your Social Media Plan

In this final section, we'll be piecing together everything discussed above and helping you to create your perfect* social media campaign.

*There's a saying that goes: "great books aren't written they're *rewritten*" (ahem). Likewise the perfect social media campaign isn't designed in one go, but honed over time as a result of testing, tweaking and retesting. Recognise that if you're new to social media there will almost certainly be a significant period of trial and error before you find the formula and approach that works best for you. In this sense then, the perfect social media campaign is built around refocus, testing and measuring results.

Your Social Media campaign needs to begin with a plan of action identifying the three key marketing elements discussed at the start of this book:

1. Your **M**essage
2. Your **M**arket
3. Your **M**ethod of communication

Your message is the basis of all that follows. It's the online identity that your company adopts and it shapes every piece of content that you publish.

The first step is to identify the goal or goals of your social media campaign from the following:

1. Directly sell more of your product or service
2. Positioning your business in your market
3. Increase awareness amongst your target audience
4. Expose yourself to a new audience
5. Encourage repeat business
6. Generate referrals
7. Give your business a personality in an otherwise bland market

Once you've got your goal specified, you need to think about the personality of the social profile. Remember that different personalities will appeal to different markets, and your social profile will essentially be the personification of your brand. So it needs to appeal to your audience whether they're penny pinchers, action-oriented fitness freaks or time-poor business owners. Note that your social personality doesn't necessarily have to *mimic* that of your audience, but should be 'one step ahead' - for example either *more* penny pinching, *more* action oriented or *even* busier.

You wouldn't expect the official Mercedes Twitter account to complain about things like "back to work on Monday morning" for example, whereas a nightclub twitter account could use this to build affinity and participate in the conversation their customers are already having in their heads: "I can't wait for the weekend and it's only 9:15 am on Monday."

As well as having a clear message and persona, you must seek to understand your market on a deep level. The reality is that after working through your message you'll likely have been thinking about your market simultaneously. Whether your target audience is a very narrow sector ('mums of children with wheat allergies' for example) or very broad ('people who buy cheap clothes'), your campaign clearly needs to appeal to the largest possible portion of your audience.

Trouble identifying or defining a market can be symptomatic of a general lack of marketing focus, and this step can sometimes prove difficult for businesses that haven't previously considered their marketing message. That's OK and it might require a longer period of study to get this finely tuned. This work can be some of the most profitable work you do, and corners shouldn't be cut in any step which involves building affinity and understanding your audience. At the same time, remember that you don't have to get it *perfect*, you just have to get it *going*. You can always adjust your course along the way.

Some questions to ask if you want to make sure that you *truly* understand your audience:
- What is their greatest fear or worry?
- What keeps them awake at night?
- What discussions are they having with their spouse or partner?
- What really drives them?

- What does their typical day look like? The narrower you can focus, the better: when do they get up? What is the first thing they do when they get to work?
- How do they perceive you and others in your industry?
- What's the preconception about your product or service? Why?

While some of these questions might seem trivial, they all help to build a really clear customer avatar in your mind. Once you have this ideal customer in mind, your marketing becomes much easier because it feels like planning a message to one person rather than a wide diverse group of people you have little affinity with.

The third planning step is to identify your method of communication, or how and where you will communicate to your audience. Each social network has a different user profile and sharing habits. The chances are that if you have similar interests to your audience you'll already have some ideas for the most relevant social networks for your business. If you don't have this insight, my recommendation would be to start doing as much as you can across Twitter, Google+ and Facebook to begin with, and see what drives the highest engagement with your audience.

Again it's important not to get caught up in the planning to the extent that actually *doing stuff* gets put off until a day in the future that never arrives. If in doubt, *do it.*

It's also worth mentioning that if you are really tuned to your audience or business, many of the points covered above will seem really intuitive and you won't have to invest much time into the planning stage. That's OK too - everyone is different and if you already know where, for whom and how your social media campaign needs to be, power to you. Hit the ground running and let's get going!

Day To Day Social Media Management

Managing your social media campaign doesn't need to be a time vampire as long as you are effective, goal-oriented and stick to the plan. The 'always on' nature and constant refreshing does mean that it's possible to spend all your time being *busy* instead of *productive*, so it's important to clearly differentiate business social media time from personal social media time.

What we usually recommend is putting aside some time each week to plan the following week's content. This allows you to get completely 'in the zone' and create or source content, write the status updates and time them to go out across the week using a tool like Hootsuite. If you see anything during the course of the week that warrants a Tweet or post, you can either bookmark it for next week's plan, or send it out as and when. You might choose to set up notifications of replies and messages, depending on how many you get and the urgency of your particular business. But having social media applications running in the background all day long constantly popping up and notifying you is a fast way to get into some unproductive habits.

To keep your distraction levels to a minimum you can check social media on breaks, during lunch and in a dedicated 'interaction' time each day.

DIY Social Media vs Outsourcing
The decision of whether to run your social media campaign yourself or outsource it is an important one. Generally we recommend that if you *want* to do it yourself, that probably means you should at least give it a go.

Some people will read this book, like the sound of what is mentioned but won't like the idea of having to do the work themselves, monitor progress and adjust course accordingly. For those people, finding someone to take care of the social media accounts on their behalf is a good idea.

Others will have the best intentions, but the reality is that once 'real life' kicks in and they are in the day to day of their business, they just won't find the time and their social media campaign will die out slowly.

If you've decided that you'd like to try social media as part of your marketing mix, it's important to be realistic about how you are going to manage this. If you do decide to outsource your social media, we can help manage your campaign. Whether you simply want

content curating and timed posts set up each week, or you're looking for a more in-depth strategy consultation, get in touch for your free social media audit and we will be happy to discuss your project and make suggestions for how we can help.

If you decide to oursource your social media elsewhere, here are some tips for choosing a provider:

- Make sure that whomever you choose understands the cultural norms in your country. A lot of outsourced social media profiles are *clearly* outsourced because the character behind the profile makes no attempt at rapport with responders. It comes across like a tiger in a gazelle costume trying to 'blend in'.
- Of course this doesn't mean you are restricted to using social media managers in your own country. The best people are able to adapt to different cultures and societies and this gives them an edge. There are significant cost savings to be made from outsourcing abroad, and we work with a worldwide team of social media managers which means our campaigns are some of the best value out there.
- Make sure that your social media outsourcer makes an effort to understand your business. There is nothing worse than a generic social profile that makes no attempt to demonstrate expertise at all. It comes across as fake and misses the point with your audience, who are looking for you to be an authority. In general, this

is often the difference between a 'good value' social media manager and one that is simply cheap. There is already enough information in the world without the need for blasting out social media messages with no additional value being added.

- Be clear about what is and isn't covered in your plan. Some outsourcers will take care of conversations with other users while others won't. Whether you decide that having someone interact with customers is a good thing or not usually depends on the level of technical complexity in your market. Doctors and dentists probably don't want someone answering patient questions on their behalf, whereas a bakery being asked questions about opening times might be glad to be relieved of having to answer such basic queries. Likewise if you want to promote original content in your campaign but you don't have the time to create this content, finding a team who have a writer on board can save you a lot of time and allow the to get on with it while you're busy running the business.

- The cheapest is not always the best value. This is especially true in marketing. Measure the numbers that are important to you (probably ROI) rather than cost. All that matters to your business is the money that social media brings in compared to what it costs. It makes no sense to artificially restrict social media budget if spending just a little more could bring in a multiple of the return. Of course you don't want to go crazy and break the bank, but pinching pennies in marketing generally shows a focus on the wrong thing - the cost - rather than the true goal - the return.

- Be wary of guarantees. Just like SEO, you'll find social media companies who are more than happy to guarantee results whether it's number of followers, increases in leads or any other metric. While it's great to be confident in one's ability to generate results, this sort of guarantee is based in an environment that they can't control and assumptions that might well prove to be erroneous. So a guarantee is usually either a sign of over optimism about 'knowing it all' or a sign that they'll do anything to make the sale. Fake followers, bought traffic, phony retweets - any metric can be gamed, so paying based on metrics is not quite as safe a bet as it might seem.

- Have realistic timescales in mind. Social Media Marketing is not as immediate as running an ad, getting significant press coverage or other transient advertising methods. If you are down to your last $100 and need customers *this week* in order to keep the lights on, there are other places you should spend that money. But if you are looking for a sustainable long-term way to generate new leads and boost sales from existing leads, social media can be a really useful component of your marketing mix.

- Have realistic expectations. Some businesses come to us expecting that top Google ranking or high social media engagement in their town or industry is the key that unlocks unlimited riches. Improvement is not enough - they want nothing short of utter transformation. But while this sort of exposure tends to be very profitable, it is not a silver bullet and increased exposure doesn't compensate for unclear marketing messages, uncompetitive offerings or an absence of any reason to buy. Social Media Marketing is one tool in your tool box, and a handy man with only one tool isn't that handy. Make sure you are putting time into the other areas of marketing your business too. See our website and other books for more information.
- Be realistic about how you'll work. Generally we find clients extremely enthusiastic to be involved in their social activity early on. Once the novelty has worn off they lose interest and the content gets more and more sporadic. If you need a manager who will be on at you every week requesting new bits of news, make sure that's what you're getting. Being effective in this situation isn't about being perfect and having no weaknesses, but understanding how you work, being realistic about your weaknesses and being honest about what it'll take to keep this thing going.
- Be wary of contracts. While it obviously takes time for the effects of any campaign to bear fruit,

you will be able to see within a couple months how effective your outsourced social media manager is. Most offer a monthly report showing the progress that is being made, so you'll have information to hand to help you decide how effective they are. Companies that work with minimum term contracts should be treated with caution as the last thing you want is to be locked into a period of working with someone who is ineffective (or worse) and forced to pay the remaining fees just to get out. We see no reason for contracts as if both parties are happy with the work being done, the relationship should continue trouble free. If the client is unhappy for any reason, they are free to go with no argument or fuss.

Next Steps

If you like what you've seen in this book, remember that we are here to answer any questions you might have. We'd also be happy to offer you a completely free of charge Online Marketing Audit - whether or not you already have social profiles set up. This audit will take a look at your existing positioning and make some suggestions about how you can use social media to position your business in your market.

To claim your free audit, head to www.exposureninja.com/audit

I really hope you've enjoyed reading this book as much as we enjoyed putting it together for you. If you have any comments, suggestions or feedback you can contact me directly tim@exposureninja.com

If you're not happy with the book in any way, I'd also like to know. I'd be happy to personally refund you the cost of the book if you don't consider it a good investment. Just drop me an email and we'll get it sorted :-)

Printed in Great Britain
by Amazon.co.uk, Ltd.,
Marston Gate.